A WORLD OF
DIFFERENCE

Yorkshire
Edited by Annabel Cook

 Young**Writers**

First published in Great Britain in 2008 by:
Young Writers
Remus House
Coltsfoot Drive
Peterborough
PE2 9JX
Telephone: 01733 890066
Website: www.youngwriters.co.uk

SB ISBN 978-1 84431 764 6

Foreword

Young Writers' Big Green Poetry Machine is a showcase for our nation's most brilliant young poets to share their thoughts, hopes and fears for the planet they call home.

Young Writers was established in 1990 to nurture creativity in our children and young adults, to give them an interest in poetry and an outlet to express themselves. Seeing their work in print will encourage them to keep writing as they grow, and become our poets of tomorrow.

Selecting the poems has been challenging and immensely rewarding. The effort and imagination invested by these young writers makes their poems a pleasure to enjoy reading time and time again.

Contents

Molly-Ann Gill (11)	20
Jenny Knott (11)	20
Katie Louise Elsom (12)	20
Reece Matthews (11)	21
Rhiannon Scott (12)	21
Jordan Bell (11)	21
Summer Crossland (12)	22
Dani Nicole Hill (12)	22
Emily Jasmine Smith (12)	23
Jack Holdsworth (12)	23
Ben Roper (12)	24
Rachel Ashton (12)	24
Hayley Chandler (12)	24
Shahnawaz Hamid (12)	25
Ronan Finch (12)	25
Damon Helliwell (12)	26
Kayleigh Whelan (12)	26
Brandon Yates (12)	27

George Pindar Community Sports College, Eastfield

James Alderton (13)	27
Bethany Kendall (13)	28
Mark Johnson (13)	28
Sam Lindley (12)	29
Bethany Singh (13)	29
Kyle Spivey	30
Tom Fordyce (13)	30
James Nicholson (13)	30
Amy Hovington (13)	31
Danni Carroll (12)	31
Nathan Egan (13)	32
Lorna Marsh (13)	32
Charlotte Draper (13)	33
Chloe Stephenson (13)	33
Lauren Price (13)	34
Charlotte Baker (12)	35
Chloe Beswick (12)	35

Handsworth Grange School, Sheffield

Imogen Stennett (12)	36

Haycliffe Special School, Bradford
Aaron Fletcher 37

Hipperholme & Lightcliffe High School, Lightcliffe
Sophie Barber (12) 38
Jake Baker (12) 38
Shaun Castle (13) 39
Emily Whitaker (12) 39
Delaney Rice (12) 40
Bethany Horner (12) 40
Chelsea Louise Elliman (12) 40
Hannah Cole (12) 41
Ryan Cunningham (12) 41
Katie Airey (11) 41
Katie Brander (11) 42
Charlotte Acton (12) 42
Jessica Wood (12) 42
Joseph Lumb (11) 43
Hannah Poulter (12) 43
Emily McCauley (12) 43
Paige Ogden (12) 44
Rhys Wardman (12) 44
Billy Thompson (11) 45
Chester Robinson (12) 45
Robert Ainley (12) 46
Sasha Louise Dale (12) 46
Laura Castle (11) 47
Sydney Stead (11) 47
Olivia Smith (11) 48
Stevie Kennedy Reed (12) 48
Faye Louise Cragon (12) 49
Andrew Rowley (11) 49
Matthew Crabtree (12) 50
Kieran Rodger (12) 50
Romana Aziz (12) 50
Olivia Burns (12) 51
Lucy Grace Thackray (12) 51

Honley High School, Honley
Ellie Charlotte Brook (12) 52
Stephen Brown (13) 53

Daniel Smith (13)	76
Josh Harper (14)	77
Callum Reaney (14)	77
Jack Phillips (14)	78

Ryedale School, Nawton
| Hannah Moody (14) | 79 |

St Pius X RC High School, Wath-upon-Dearne
Christopher King (13)	80
Benn Dirienzo (14)	81
Abbie Easton (12)	81
Lewis Lynch (14)	81
Lorenzo Camattari (14)	82
Holly Sheridan (14)	82
Daniel Chapman (14)	83
Lucy Staniforth (14)	83
Matthew Blakeley (14)	84
Georgina Brett (13)	84
Grace Ackroyd (14)	84
Oliver Ward (14)	85
Alex Richardson (14)	85
Dom Howell (13)	85
Abigail Cotton (14)	86
Bradley Peake (14)	86
Olivia Pratt (14) & Louis Staniforth (13)	87
Andy Deng (12)	87
Connor Patrick Hale (14)	88
Matthew Burgin (13)	88
Conor Cronly (14)	89
Hayley Burke (11)	89
Emily Hague (12)	90
Lauren Poole (13)	90
Chad Bronson (14)	91
John Shaw (13)	91
Shannon Sarah Simpson (13)	92

Spen Valley Sports College, Liversedge
Hamza Nawaz (13)	92
Kirsty Butterworth (13)	92
Samuel Humpleby (12)	93

Rebecca Todd (12)	93
Kristoffer John Parker (13)	93
Leonie Jaye Horne (13)	94
Connor Ellis (13)	94
Avon Blyth (13)	95
Jennifer Newsome & Charlotte Day (13)	95
Josh Cutler (13)	96
Sarah Firth (13)	96
Fraser Laycock (12)	97
Elliott Hirst (13)	97
Charlotte Coates (13)	98
Jack Booker (12)	98

Swinton Community School, Mexborough

Chloé McMullan (13)	99
Cole Tolley (13)	99
Luke Allen (13)	100
Jessica Rowley (13)	100
Millie Clamp (12)	100
Samuel Bennett (12)	101
Lewis Creamer (13)	101
Thomas Drew (12)	102
Paige Gelder (13)	102
Lauren Cooper (12)	103
Sophie Barnett (13)	103
Zoe Brain (13)	104
Joshua Bell (12)	104
Yeorgia Argirou (12)	105
Christopher Birks (13)	105
Hannah Roebuck (13)	106
Bradley-Allen Sharp (13)	106
Katie Parkin (12)	107

The King's School, Pontefract

Ben Liddle (12)	107
Heather Tonks (13)	107
Lucy Hill (12)	108
Olivia Mountain (13)	108
Kate Maeer (13)	109
Ryan Kaye (12)	109
Jack Hiorns (11)	110

The Poems

What Right Have We?

What right have we
To chop down the tees?
These ancient tall giants
Covering species unseen.

The sleek, regal panther
Enjoying the sun,
The bright-feathered macaw,
Are their days finally done?

We're drowning in plastic,
Our Earth is warming up,
The clouds drop deadly acid,
Can anything be done?

The answer lies before us,
Deep within our heads,
For starters no more rubbish,
Let's use paper bags instead.

We must protect our trees
And the animals and the seas,
After all some plants can even cure disease!
You do not have to listen,
But I sincerely hope you do,
For everything that affects the Earth
Affects me and even you!

Rebecca Wright (13)
Brantwood School, Sheffield

What If?

What if I had no control, no power?
I start to think of a matter which makes me feel sour,
I think in depth and then I dread,
What if I was virtually dead?
What if I had no idea what fate had in store for me?
That if I had no existing family?
That if I had no shelter, no place I could call home?
What if I had no freedom, no place to roam?

What if, what if, what if?

Sarah McCloskey (12)
Brantwood School, Sheffield

Look Around

Let's sit down and look to the future,
Look into your crystal ball.
Does what you see fill you with delight?
A sky full of birds, a spectacular sight!
Or does what you see hold you with dread?

We sat down and thought of the future,
We sat down with no crystal ball,
What we saw now holds us with delight,
A future for all animals has got to be the perfect sight.

Alexandra Savage (13)
Brantwood School, Sheffield

Litter, Litter On The Ground

Litter, litter on the ground
Some places where it can't be found
You can pick it up and put it in the bin
Even if it's a rotten tin
If it's on a street or next to your feet
Just pick it up and put it in the bin.

Carianne Oakley (12)
Bruntcliffe High School, Morley

The Silent Killer

Smoking is horrible,
Very, very smelly, pooh!
Smoke reaches out and grabs you,
It likes to move around swiftly,
Swish, swosh,
Coughing, spluttering,
It just wants more.

Drinking is horrible,
Very strong, grr!
Sliding down your throat,
Making you act stupid,
It just wants more.

Drugs are horrible,
Very, very addictive, more, more!
Buy it in a needle,
Buy it in a sachet,
Makes you act dumb and daft.

Don't even try these,
You could even die,
Just say no!
It won't make you cry.
The silent killers.

Shannon Lockwood (12)
Bruntcliffe High School, Morley

Animal Cruelty

Every minute of the day,
One little animal wastes away.
It's not fair and it's not nice,
So if you're caught you will pay a price.
You could be fined or even jailed.
It's always like the animals have failed.
They're poor and helpless everywhere,
We need your help to keep them there!

Keara Whelan (12)
Bruntcliffe High School, Morley

Poverty

Sick and starving in this world,
A life not good for you or me.
It makes our lives full of woe
And tears are coming for us to see.

Starving is bad, no good in it all,
The world goes down like a big block wall.
Starvation comes and finally death,
Why is this world in such a mess?

The sick, poor, helpless and weak,
There's nothing they can do.
Feeling so weak,
We've got to help, it's something we can do.

Charities seem so helpful and good,
Just how they really should.
But some people hold money back,
These greedy people make poverty last.

Debbie Lee Thacker (11)
Bruntcliffe High School, Morley

The Darkness Falling

The darkness falling,
A blanket of death,
Sending people sleepy,
Like a hypnotist.
It doesn't come out
Unless the sun is out of sight,
The evil creatures come out to fight.
The sun comes out and they're out of sight,
Then the darkness is falling again,
The cycle starts again.

Bethany Waite (12)
Bruntcliffe High School, Morley

The Devil's Dream

Bang! goes a gun, with a silver bullet
A sickening thud and a crack to the skull.
There, yet another body seized
And another soul stolen.
War is a demon, a soul stealer.
Boom! A blast, down falls a building,
You hear repetitive screaming,
Mothers weeping, sirens bleeping.
Crash! Building after building falls,
Bodies lying in the streets, torn, helpless.
War's laughing. Sniggering at you,
Then silence.
The streets are abandoned,
Guns left lying around.
Whoosh! From above two planes,
A hatch opens from beneath, two objects drop.
Bang! All is gone and all is lost forever.
War is the Devil's dream.

Chantelle Louise Potter (12)
Bruntcliffe High School, Morley

Floating

Floating, alone, abandoned.
What did I do?
Homeless.
There are more of us.
We keep building up.
Soon it will be too late.
Lost in a world of litter.
The wars on the street a problem.
The war against litter - disastrous.
Used then abused.

Ben Bousfield (13)
Bruntcliffe High School, Morley

Litter, Litter Everywhere

Litter, litter on the ground
Litter, litter all around
If there's a bin, put it in
Don't commit an awful sin
If you see a can on the floor
Don't just go through your door
If there's a bin, put it in
If you see someone littering tell them off
And if they scoff tell them off
If you see a crisp packet
Pick it up
If there's a bin, put it in
If your bin is full to bursting
Put it in your pocket
And when you find a bin
Put it in.

Harry Ferguson (12)
Bruntcliffe High School, Morley

Flowers

Flowers on the street,
Flowers on the road,
Flowers so neat,
Along comes a toad.

Splat go the flowers on the street,
Splat go the flowers on the road,
Splat go the flowers so neat,
Now there's only a toad.

Beth Roper (12)
Bruntcliffe High School, Morley

Bye-Bye Birdie

There's a seal - *wallop*!
That will be a nice leather coat.

Look - a whale!
Bang goes the harpoon gun.
The whale struggles.
Bang! that's another harpoon,
That will be a nice piece of meat.

Chop, chop, that's a monkey's home gone,
Or maybe a bird's nest.
All for a piece of paper.

Puff puff, that is a smoker
Trying to extinct us all.

Jamie Bentley (12)
Bruntcliffe High School, Morley

Iraqi War

Gun shot
Bombs drop
Too many people have had to go.
Emotions are on for show.
All they want is to know
Where their loved ones are.
Drink your worries away
At the bar.
Loved ones matter,
Tears go pitter-patter.
Don't worry,
Stay strong for your children.

Elliot Jennings (12)
Bruntcliffe High School, Morley

Where Are The Dolphins? - Going, Going, Gone

Do you think of the dolphin
While you're busy golfing?
The ones that are choking on all the plastic bags
Thrown in by all the wags
You may be thinking whatever, whatever, but never, never
It is now time to take action

Do you think of all the dolphins getting caught in the fish nets
While you are making bets?
Just so you can have fish and chips and all your seafood dips
You may be thinking whatever, whatever, but never, never
It is now time to take action

So we must stop this now, before it is too late
And not using the poor dolphins as bait
Stop, stop, stop, it's time to take action
Hold that rubbish and bin your pot
And help us save the dolphins!

Lauren Taylor (12)
Bruntcliffe High School, Morley

Disappearing Ice

Blocks of ice fall into the sea
The poor polar bear thinks, *what could it be?*
They're perfectly innocent, they've done nothing wrong
In about 50 years these great bears will be gone

They mind their own business, just stay on the snow
The ozone's disappearing, but they do not know
They're going to be extinct, it's not because of them
Their world is disappearing from underneath them
It's 'cause of us they're going extinct
And when they're safe I'll stop moaning then.

Shane Aveyard (13)
Bruntcliffe High School, Morley

The Unfairness Of Life

Sat in their hospital beds,
Wishing they were never born,
Praying that God will help them,
Hating him or her for this happening to them,
Through no fault of their own.
They were given this terrible disease,
Having people crying on their shoulders
Day in and day out.
Think how it would feel -
Like you can't get out.

So live life like there's no tomorrow,
You never know what's coming around the corner,
Live, laugh, love.
Ignore the people that try to bring you down.
Just be grateful
This very poem
Is not about you!

Elena Fernandez-Moreno (12)
Bruntcliffe High School, Morley

Poverty's Taking Over

Life won't be worth living,
Dusty rocks and cobble streets.
Dreams will never be lived,
If they could die . . . they'd die.
If they could live a better life . . . they would.
It isn't you sat there, watching people die slowly,
Think, donate!
Help them survive!

Shelbi Hoole (12)
Bruntcliffe High School, Morley

Where's The Animals?

Animals, animals, animals,
Birds and bears and bats.
Animals, animals, animals,
Pandas and big cats.

Animals disappearing,
Less and less each day
And us as people of the Earth
Have to save them in every way.

Animals, animals, animals,
Rhinos and hippos and sharks,
Animals, animals, animals,
Vultures are ever so dark.

Poachers are chasing animals
With guns and spears and nets.
Animals run away, terrified,
But killing's what poachers do best.

Stop them, stop them,
Before it's too late . . .
The animals need our help,
Cos now they've been caught,
using the poacher's bait.

Emma Hudson (12)
Bruntcliffe High School, Morley

Animals . . .

Abandoned on the street
They're hungry, they're cold
And want someone to hold
Not a lot left
No one really cares
So get up now
'Cause you know how
Before they're all gone!

Nat Denton (13)
Bruntcliffe High School, Morley

Litter Is Bitter

There was a boy
Who talked a lot,
He had a toy
That made a noise.

He didn't like it,
So he threw it,
Onto the floor
And left it there.

It didn't disintegrate,
It didn't go,
But it stayed there
Forever and ever.

A person came
And picked it up,
The person kept it,
To make it good.

So now you know,
Not to litter,
Because it stays there,
Forever and ever.

Bethany Avison (12)
Bruntcliffe High School, Morley

Litter

I littered once
I littered twice
And now I have to pay the price
I pick up things I once did throw
I put them in a bag that seems to grow and grow
So think again before you litter
You can make the world a whole lot fitter
So come on people, don't be bitter.

Emily Wardle (13)
Bruntcliffe High School, Morley

Terrorism

There's terrorism in the world
We need heroism in the world
Swap guns for roses
We don't need poses
Terrorist bombers attacking the world
9/11 and London bombings all are evil
There's no need for this, it just takes the mick
All they need is a kick
In the right direction for correction
Misunderstood, bombs in the pub, it's all wrong
It's gone on for too long, *bang!*
They need a new life, let's stop the fight
Osama bin Laden and Saddam Hussein
Are all playing this game
They do it for fame
But really it's a shame
So stop!

Jack Robinson (12)
Bruntcliffe High School, Morley

What Is Different?

Black and white, pink or blue,
what is the difference between me and you?
They're all just colours,
But a person is about the heart, the soul.
So why, oh why, do we hurt people's feelings
And judge them by the colour of their skin?
We need to fight it and let us reunite
Before it gets worse and starts a massive fight.
War after war, religion against religion,
So let us be friends
And turn all this madness to joy and gladness.

Kieran Laverick (12)
Bruntcliffe High School, Morley

Stop The Bullies

Bullying, bullying is the worst,
Bullying, bullying makes everyone's waterworks burst.

They make you cry,
I don't know why, but they think that they're the best
And better than all the rest.
They think they're strong
But they are wrong.

They make you cry,
I don't know why,
But think they are the best,
Better than all the rest.

They won't stop it,
You should tell them to drop it
And leave you alone.

Steve Tempest (12)
Bruntcliffe High School, Morley

Crime Is Bad

C rime makes the world a bad place
R acism doesn't make you cool
I hate crime
M onsters are people who do the crime
E vil is what they are

I s crime bad? Do you think so? I know I do.
S exual abuse is really unfair

B urning things is very dangerous
A rson is what it's called
D eath is caused by other people a lot - murder.

Adam Tootill (12)
Bruntcliffe High School, Morley

Recycling Is Cool

Recycling is cool,
Don't be a fool,
Don't sin the bin,
Put it in.

Please don't litter,
The world will be bitter,
So if you want to fit in
Put it in the bin.

Green is good,
Green is best,
In the green bin
Your rubbish will rest.

Corey White (11)
Bruntcliffe High School, Morley

Human? Cow? You Decide

Are you a human?
Are you a cow?
Live on a farm
Or in a house?

Well start acting like it then
Put your litter in the bin
Keep your world a tidy place
It's not just mine or yours
Or his or hers
It's all of ours
So spread the word
And save the world!

Maizy Griffiths (12)
Bruntcliffe High School, Morleylots And Lots Of Litter

The Earth Is Ending

First of all we need O_2
And plants need CO_2.
Enough suffering,
Enough suffering,
Natural disasters,
How much paper has been wasted
By all these familiar faces?
Trees cut,
Trees cut,
Falling to the ground,
Falling to the ground.
Which bin, which bin
To put it in?
Which one,
Which one,
For my litter,
For my litter?
I'm scared of this,
Hold me close,
Crashing,
Crashing,
Banging,
Banging,
Boom!
What was that noise?
Where am I now?
Boom! Boom! I warned you,
The Earth is gone.
Boom!

Olivia Talbot (11)
Bruntcliffe High School, Morley

Terrorism

I hate terrorists making a boom.
They should all be locked in a tomb.
I am sitting and feeling sad,
I dislike them, they are bad.
They make bombs from petrol and gas,
Trying to blow up any old lass.
I think about 9/11,
Sending people to God's Heaven.
Some of these are sent to jail,
But most of them are let out on bail.
Lots of people getting killed,
Lots of people injured and chilled.
They do it just for attention
If they were in school I'd put them in detention.
I am near the end of my rhyme,
I think now is the right time.

Ryan Hanson (12)
Bruntcliffe High School, Morley

Recyclable

Recycle, recycle, only some people do it.
Put a plastic bottle away and reuse it another day.
Recycle, recycle, it's good to do today.

If a tree was planted for every one cut down
There would be about the same amount of trees in the world
So recycle paper to save trees.

Do you like cans? Recycle them
Because you might have the same can again and again.
It's the beginning of recycling so do it.

Macaulay Taylor (12)
Bruntcliffe High School, Morley

War

War is a terrible thing,
People dying, bombs flying,
Ground is frying.

We all hate it,
It's very sad,
It also makes us very mad.

The Nazis are here to kill,
Our ration card is like a bill,
Run away if you don't want to die
In the explosions,
Your skin will fry.

Look out!
Here's the nuclear bomb!
Soon we will all be gone.

James Nassau (11)
Bruntcliffe High School, Morley

War

Boom goes the gun
Bang goes the fun
Everywhere is dull
If they bring the war to Hull

Bang goes an enemy
Boom goes another
That's when he found out
It was his brother
From another mother.

Jacob Flathers (11)
Bruntcliffe High School, Morley

Global Warming And Pollution

The cars that are so ugly
Destroying air that's so lovely

When we light the coal
We're melting the North Pole

The electricity you waste
Don't say you forgot
You're making the world hot

Smoking and doing drugs isn't good
Soon it will cause the worst floods

So before you waste electricity
Halt!
And make global warming not your fault.

Troy Lawrence (12)
Bruntcliffe High School, Morley

War Of The Animals

The screams of animals in the night.
The screams of animals are a fright!
As we murder, as we kill,
The squeals of animals are a chill!
The lion went mad and killed the king,
There's one thing he wants, just one thing.
He wants a friend to love and care,
Someone to love and be there.
But we do not know, as we cannot hear,
So the animals' minds, they fill with fear!

Harry Haley (12)
Bruntcliffe High School, Morley

The Fight For The Earth

The Earth comes out, looking scared
But Global Warming is determined,
Earth strikes first,
Trees,
Flowers,
Grass,
Global Warming doesn't even flinch
And Global Warming doesn't hesitate to fight back,
Greenhouse gas,
Spray cans,
Cars,
Factories.
Earth jumps back and gives it everything he's got,
Recycling,
Rainforests,
Bottle banks,
Walking.
Global Warming felt those hits,
But still fights back,
Litter,
Melting ice caps,
Pollution,
Nuclear waste.
Earth is down and isn't getting up
And Global Warming is the champion.

Luke Sugden (11)
Bruntcliffe High School, Morley

Being Homeless

Being homeless is really bad,
It will make you feel really sad,
You will get no food,
Some of the nights will be cruel,
A cardboard box will be your home
And every night you will be alone.
Please end this gormless fright
And make these people warm at night.

Molly-Ann Gill (11)
Bruntcliffe High School, Morley

My World

I have created a world which is the best place to be,
Beautiful rainbows, no poverty, my world is clean with no litter.
So I speak for people in the world,
Change litter into glitter.
My world is a good place,
We don't stand racism,
Saying things that aren't nice to people,
The way they look.
So I think you should all shut up!

Jenny Knott (11)
Bruntcliffe High School, Morley

Hunger

Hungriness and emptiness is all I feel
The sun goes down and the moon comes up
But I sit there hoping and praying
I will get some food, until one day
I can bear it no longer
I freeze and perish and slowly wither away
Into *nothingness*
All because of *hungriness*.

Katie Louise Elsom (12)
Bruntcliffe High School, Morley

War

The screeches and crashes of the tanks rolling in,
Our little army knowing we're not going to win.
And there is me, just one little boy,
Sat there, alone, with my one friendly toy.
My parents have gone and just left me,
I sometimes wonder just how they will be.
Now the fighting has started, the death and the pain
And there I am, just sat there in vain.
When the banging got closer they burst through the door,
Glass and debris shattered all over the floor.

Reece Matthews (11)
Bruntcliffe High School, Morley

Today's The Day

Litter, litter, it's cluttering our world.
Litter, litter, it's disgusting and gross.
Litter, litter, let's clean it up.
Litter, litter, come and help us.
Litter, litter, it's going away.
Let's make that day today!

Rhiannon Scott (12)
Bruntcliffe High School, Morley

Death Day

The continuous noise of screaming,
As the enemy are cheering,
As the sky turns black,
As the enemy gets the last laugh,
As the bodies lay down,
Not making a sound,
As the enemy cheers,
He can tell his last breath is near.

Jordan Bell (11)
Bruntcliffe High School, Morley

Clean Up Your Act

Not so long ago
In a town known as Disgusting
She sits on the floor
Dropping litter more and more!
She is ruining the town
She makes them frown
Why can't she see
She just thinks like you and me
She will just keep walking past it all
Thinking that the problem is small
It's not
It will get worse
If you will - she might.

Summer Crossland (12)
Bruntcliffe High School, Morley

Is It Art?

Spraying paint
On a plain blank wall
Staining your city
Does it make you feel tall?

Now your actions
Have come to this
Was it worth it
Now you're nicked?

Do you criticise
Those who take part
Or recognise
This crime is *art!*

Dani Nicole Hill (12)
Bruntcliffe High School, Morley

CO$_2$ Emissions

CO$_2$ emissions
Makes many decisions
Whether to go by car
Or walk, it's not too far.
The ozone layer is getting thin,
It's like us losing aging skin.
The Earth is getting way too hot,
If you're happy - I'm not.
For future generations to see a polar bear,
Do you think it matters - do you really care?
Do you want some time to spend
Or do you want the world to end?

Emily Jasmine Smith (12)
Bruntcliffe High School, Morley

Extinction

Life and death, life and death,
Down to the depths,
Found far away,
Or hiding for another day.

Animals find their way,
During night and day.
But they can't guarantee
That they'll come home with some tea.

Boom, boom, boom,
Running to their doom,
Are they still alive
Or are they taking a mighty dive?

Jack Holdsworth (12)
Bruntcliffe High School, Morley

Crime Or Art?

Graffiti skull on the wall
Graffiti writing marking territory
Some people call it art
But others just say not.

People spraying on my door
We want more, more, more!
Spray, spray, spray, spray,
Round the park we go.

Ben Roper (12)
Bruntcliffe High School, Morley

Litter, litter everywhere

Litter, litter in the air
Litter, litter on the ground
Litter, litter still being found

Dropping litter must stop
So please don't drop
Put your litter in the bin
And save the world for your kin.

Rachel Ashton (12)
Bruntcliffe High School, Morley

Health

H ealth in our world needs help
E veryone join together
A nd be a good Samaritan
L et them live their lives to the full
T ell everyone to help
H ealth is a problem, help them please!

Hayley Chandler (12)
Bruntcliffe High School, Morley

Drugs World

The world is in danger
In danger of sins
In danger of drugs
Such as steroids and heroin.

Steroids cause aggression
Murder and pain
What's the need for these drugs?
Why play this game?

LSD is no better
Makes you see things that aren't here
It's no good to the world
It only causes fear.

Heroin's the same
Evil and dreadful
We don't need this drugs world
I prefer the normal one.

Shahnawaz Hamid (12)
Bruntcliffe High School, Morley

Just Do It

The world is packed with litter
The world is packed with rubbish
On the streets it lays about, growing every day
It makes the world a disgusting place
Yes, so, what a disgrace!
People throw it there
People throw it everywhere
But mostly they do not care
So put it in the bin
It's such a small thing
So come on folks, don't be dumb
Pull out your thumb
Just do it!

Ronan Finch (12)
Bruntcliffe High School, Morley

Extinction

Extinction, extinction all around me
Birds are falling out of the trees
Monkeys are dying
We're not trying
To save the monkeys

Stop the killing
It's not fulfilling
The animals are going away
So why should we stay?

Damon Helliwell (12)
Bruntcliffe High School, Morley

Greed

All the greed in the world is taking charge.
The wealthy people just don't care about the poor.
The greed starts in America and England of course.
We just don't care about the poor in countries quite large.
But that is where Fairtrade comes in,
Making everyone equal and everyone will win.
Giving the right amount of money to people and their crops,
Just by paying a little more money
For the things in our shops.

Kayleigh Whelan (12)
Bruntcliffe High School, Morley

Graffiti

Graffiti, graffiti
A serious crime
Graffiti, graffiti
A sign of our time
Graffiti, graffiti
Is it art?
Graffiti, graffiti
Comes from the heart
Graffiti, graffiti
Printed on the walls
Graffiti, graffiti
The walls have to fall
Graffiti, graffiti
It looks so nice
Graffiti, graffiti
But you pay the price
Graffiti, graffiti
Cheap and nasty
Graffiti, graffiti
Unfortunately it lasts.

Brandon Yates (12)
Bruntcliffe High School, Morley

Deforestation - Haikus

Deforestation
A terrible thing to do
Please help the forest

Non-sentient trees
The chainsaw is warm in death
But still they are dead.

James Alderton (13)
George Pindar Community Sports College, Eastfield

Differences

People think poverty is abroad,
The truth is it's here, in the UK.
It's everywhere we go,
People living, homeless, on the street,
Not earning enough to live, eat or sleep.
I can make a difference.

Global warming is everywhere,
You hear it in the news.
The planet's getting hotter,
Icebergs are melting.
Recycle is the big word,
Listen to it.
We can make a difference.

Animals come in all shapes and sizes,
Fluffy, hairy, big and small.
But soon they will all be gone,
No more four-legged creatures.
They will only be seen
In books and magazines.
You can make a difference!

Bethany Kendall (13)
George Pindar Community Sports College, Eastfield

Amazon

A mazing mythical creatures
M ay live and look the same
A ll of them are famous
Z oos hold a few of them
O n the brink of extinction
N o one really cares.

Mark Johnson (13)
George Pindar Community Sports College, Eastfield

World War II

What have they done to this beautiful land?
Animals and wildlife have been destroyed.
So many lives have been lost for nothing.
Just for the cruel pleasure of victory.
Children separated from their parents.
Millions of pounds spent on explosives.
I have been talking about World War II.
Sending in hundreds of troops to die,
All because of someone's selfishness.
Someday the wildlife will be restored
And happiness will be brought back worldwide.
We will eventually get back life.
Pray to God that genocide won't come back.
Pray to God that World War III never comes.

Sam Lindley (12)
George Pindar Community Sports College, Eastfield

In The Future

Forests will be gone, like in my dreams.
It will be coming true soon it should seem.
Will children get to see nests high in trees?
They may not even get to see a bee.

The weather is now a mess, we are to blame.
Dying animals scattered everywhere.
For example - a giant polar bear!
Look at your surroundings, what do you see?
Something that will just be a momory!

Look at our world and think how you can help.
Maybe recycling is the place to start.
Then you can do more things for the planet.
This poem is to help our planet!

Bethany Singh (13)
George Pindar Community Sports College, Eastfield

Warfare

Stop war
People are dying
Lots of people sitting and crying
People get shot dead
Straight through their head
Watching, waiting, in the trenches
They could be sitting on park benches
Bullets are firing
Lots of guns
They all weigh up to a hundred tons.

Kyle Spivey
George Pindar Community Sports College, Eastfield

Gangs

Gang crime increases
As do the members.
People die like the safety of the citizens.
Gangsters worried about the guns they use
And detectives finding clues.

Tom Fordyce (13)
George Pindar Community Sports College, Eastfield

Iraq

I mpossible to overrule.
R uining our world,
A lways in the headlines,
Q uarreling with each other.

James Nicholson (13)
George Pindar Community Sports College, Eastfield

Save The World From Destruction

The trees are green
The sky is blue
But not for much longer
As pollution pumps through

The sea creatures are big and small
But not for much longer
As trash kills all

The wind and the rain, heavy and light
Much more of that
As floods give fright

So time to save the world
From devastation
Before it ruins our great nation.

Amy Hovington (13)
George Pindar Community Sports College, Eastfield

Polar Bears

Save the poor bears.
Take some care.

It makes them mad,
Which turns them sad.

Save the deep
And make it keep.

Make a plan
Build a dam.

Save the polar bears,
Take some care!

Danni Carroll (12)
George Pindar Community Sports College, Eastfield

Environment

Baby animals die every day
Because in our environment,
Our animals' habitats
We are destroying that.

Other animals are already dead and extinct.
Many animals are dying out
Because we are taking away their homes and food.

So please, help all the animals
For your sake.

Nathan Egan (13)
George Pindar Community Sports College, Eastfield

Wildlife Poem

Wildlife all around
Searching deep, into the ground
As they leap around
Please help save the animals
They do no harm
Most of them are only little
And calm.

Bunnies, as white as snow
Fluffy and bouncy, they flow
Leaping around like kangaroos
Help these animals in their zoo.

Lorna Marsh (13)
George Pindar Community Sports College, Eastfield

Save The Trees!

Please help the green
As pollution is mean.

Save the melting ice
Do something nice.

Cut down on fuel
Keep the planet cool.

It is very sad
As it makes people mad.

Save the trees
And let the planet breathe.

Stop using paper
Or no trees later!

Charlotte Draper (13)
George Pindar Community Sports College, Eastfield

Litter

Litter, litter all around
On the floor, on the ground
Simply place it in a bin
Because you'll know it's not a sin
Recycle, be green and be clean
Even though you won't get paid a bean
Now the Earth is nice and clean
Keep it up, c'mon, it's easy
Easy, easy, easy-peasy.

Chloe Stephenson (13)
George Pindar Community Sports College, Eastfield

What It's Like To Be Abused

Alone in the dark,
Crying for help,
Unwanted and useless,
That's what my parents say.

Scared and depressed,
I can only feel pain,
Helpless and unloved,
No food, no drink.

School is as bad,
Bullied and no friends,
'You were a mistake,' they say,
Then it's home time.

I'm not looking forward to going home,
I dawdle home,
But I am late,
I get punched and kicked.

Tea is a slice of bread,
Cheese and a drink of water,
No TV, no music,
Straight to bed I go, no goodnight hug.

And this is how I live every day,
Alone, depressed and upset,
I cry myself to sleep,
Then it's the same as yesterday.

And it goes around
Again and again . . .

Lauren Price (13)
George Pindar Community Sports College, Eastfield

Animals And Extinction

Animals will soon be extinct,
The animals - from our planet,
All because of food.
To be rich,
Living on top of the world.

Next we have food, meaning meat,
You know, the things we eat,
From the animals we keep.

But it's not all a long and happy life
For most animals,
As they are stuffed
And packed into huts.

Charlotte Baker (12)
George Pindar Community Sports College, Eastfield

Extinction

Extinction, it is happening to all animals,
Dying out because of things all around.
Hunting, money and food we need,
Our animals will soon be extinct.

Pandas, polar bears, tigers,
All around there will only be pictures soon enough.
There will be no animals left in the world,
It's entirely up to us.

Global warming, pollution and death,
It's all because of us.
Our children will want to see them,
So help the animals of the world.

Chloe Beswick (12)
George Pindar Community Sports College, Eastfield

Why Me?

People call me nasty names,
Just because I'm black.
They try to play evil games,
But I can't do them back.

My mum says I'm bubbly,
My dad says I'm cool.
But people call me fat and ugly
And they also call me a fool.

There's a girl in my class,
She's got rashes on her face,
She's a lovely lass,
But she's a disgrace.

So why does it have to be me?
Is it because I'm black?
I wish people would let me free!
I wish I could pay them back!

Why me?

Imogen Stennett (12)
Handsworth Grange School, Sheffield

Writing About Litter

Paper, bottles, plastic, cans,
Crisp packets, boxes and elastic bands.
These are the things that go in bins,
But some don't.
Oh, what a dump.
Some litter is just left there,
Some kills animals,
Oh, what a scare.
Don't make the street a mess,
Pick up the litter, that's the best.
Keep it nice, keep it clean,
Soon we'll see
That the streets will gleam.

Bins are all kinds of colours and shapes.
Pick up the litter and then you will say,
The street is in tip-top shape.

Please,
Pick up the litter
And make the world
A whole lot bigger.

Aaron Fletcher
Haycliffe Special School, Bradford

Save The Planet

S ome people take note of the news
A nd recycle their rubbish, but
V ery silly people ignore it and think it doesn't matter
E very day the ice caps melt and

T he polar bears get trapped and die.
H ot weather makes the ice melt
E ven if we recycle we need to turn off our lights as well

P layStations are left on for no reason at all
L ots of televisions are left on standby
A nd lights are left on
N ot everybody is as selfish and turn their lights off
E veryone can help save the planet
T he planet is dying, so help!

Sophie Barber (12)
Hipperholme & Lightcliffe High School, Lightcliffe

Recycle Man

He's got green blood running through his veins,
He's still working to stop freak rains.
He keeps polar bears alive,
He helps endangered species thrive.
We could be like him,
Instead of putting recyclable things in the bin.
We need to try to save the rainforest as much as we can,
Otherwise you'll end up with a red tan.
If we don't start recycling we will have floods
And if we don't we'll always wear hoods.
He will recycle metal cans,
He's super duper Recycle Man!

Jake Baker (12)
Hipperholme & Lightcliffe High School, Lightcliffe

Difference

Arctic seals and polar bears,
Orang-utans and frogs.
We are all one big machine,
Each of us a cog.
We can make a difference.

A fact of life is deforestation,
One lone person cannot stop it.
Only when we are united as a nation
Can the way forward be lit.
We can make a difference.

Recycle and save power,
Walk to work and use what you need.
We can stop global warming,
Together we can succeed.
You can make a difference!

Shaun Castle (13)
Hipperholme & Lightcliffe High School, Lightcliffe

Extinction

E lephants are dying
eX tra care is taken
T o try and make things better
I n this big mistake
N ever stop trying
C rying doesn't help
T hough it makes you feel better
I n this big mistake
O xygen breathes the air of life
N ever stop trying because the world is dying.

Emily Whitaker (12)
Hipperholme & Lightcliffe High School, Lightcliffe

Recycle

R ecycle leftover things
E at your food
C are and recycle
Y ou need to save electricity
C yle to work
L ights - turn them off
E lectricity needs to be turned off.

Delaney Rice (12)
Hipperholme & Lightcliffe High School, Lightcliffe

Whales

W e swim all day through the deep blue sea
H aving fun with our friends
A lthough not many are left
L ife is changing all the time for us
E ven ending for some
S o help me save my friends.

Bethany Horner (12)
Hipperholme & Lightcliffe High School, Lightcliffe

Whales

W e swim with our friends down below
H aving such fun
A lthough we lose our friends and their souls
L ittle has been said
E very bit we hear will stay in our minds
S o sad, we lost them, they will stay in our hearts.
    Save them today!

Chelsea Louise Elliman (12)
Hipperholme & Lightcliffe High School, Lightcliffe

Help, Help, Pollution

Can you help stop pollution
It might be your New Year's resolution
Restaurants, buses, trains and more
Picking up litter might be a bore
Pick up litter, cans and more
It might wash up on the shore
Help, help stop pollution, please.

Hannah Cole (12)
Hipperholme & Lightcliffe High School, Lightcliffe

Animal

Animals are dying like the humpback whale and polar bears
Nature being chopped down, like the rainforest in Brazil
Important to stop using up lots of electricity as the world is heating up
Aardvarks are going extinct, so stop cutting down their habitat
Long term thinking of going green,
Stop thinking and go green now.

Ryan Cunningham (12)
Hipperholme & Lightcliffe High School, Lightcliffe

How To Help The World

When you go to bed at night, turn out the light.
Animals are dying, so stop flying to Spain or France.
Cycle to school, don't use your car,
If you don't drive very far.
Turn off the telly at night or the world will be a horrible sight.
Save the world.

Katie Airey (11)
Hipperholme & Lightcliffe High School, Lightcliffe

Go Green

G et started on going green
O ur televisions tell us to . . .

G et out our energy saving light bulbs
R ecycle glass, plastic, paper and clothes
E xtinction is happening
E nd all of this by . . .
N ever leaving electricity on.
    Go green!

Katie Brander (11)
Hipperholme & Lightcliffe High School, Lightcliffe

Go Green

G o green and save our planet
O ur world is getting hotter

G oing out, why not walk instead of taking your car
R ecycling helps a lot more than you think
E verything in the world matters
E ven turning off your TV
N othing else matters, so go green.

Charlotte Acton (12)
Hipperholme & Lightcliffe High School, Lightcliffe

Recycle

Please recycle, don't be mean,
Don't panic, just go green.
Think about the green grass
And look at all that recyclable glass.
Try not to waste a light,
Turn it off in the night.
Just think about the Polar caps,
Turn off all your leaking taps.

Jessica Wood (12)
Hipperholme & Lightcliffe High School, Lightcliffe

The Ill Old Man

The ozone layer, just like an old man losing his hair.
He's weak and frail, he has a hard life -
The pollution of Earth has pushed through,
Just like being stabbed with a knife.
He has been crucified by the odd person leaving on a light bulb
Or switch, but if we could care,
Reach out and grab the old man out of his chair,
Then we could protect our planet's ozone layer.

Joseph Lumb (11)
Hipperholme & Lightcliffe High School, Lightcliffe

Recycle And Save

Recycle your paper and your cans
Reuse your glass, handwash your pans.

Turn your washer to 30°, don't use your car
Only wash if dirty, only to travel very far.

Like the grass the Earth will be green
With just one bottle you can live the dream.

Hannah Poulter (12)
Hipperholme & Lightcliffe High School, Lightcliffe

Recycling

Recycling can be a tricky thing,
But just think of all the good it can bring.
So put some rubbish in the bin,
Glass, paper and plastic too
This helps the world and also you.

Save the planet and yourself too,
So what else can you do?

Emily McCauley (12)
Hipperholme & Lightcliffe High School, Lightcliffe

Making The World A Better Place

Love would make the world a better place
Of this there is a small trace
If there were no pollution the air would be pure
For this there is a cure, I'm sure
Violence hits our streets each day
I wish it all would go away
Litter, litter everywhere
No one even stops to care
Homeless people living rough
No one seems to do enough
Picking up rubbish and helping others
Sticking together like sisters and brothers
Love would make the world a better place
Of this there is a small trace.

Paige Ogden (12)
Hipperholme & Lightcliffe High School, Lightcliffe

Help The World

The ice caps are melting fast,
So reduce your CO^2 at last.
Fumes are puncturing the ozone layer
And are letting in the sun's harmful flares.
Walk instead of drive,
Or catch a bus, you'll let the oxygen survive.
Make power stations a thing of the past,
Use less energy, it's not a hard task.
Smoke is harmful to the world,
The atmosphere is being blurred.
So help stop climate change
And you won't be the one to blame.
So finish the pollution,
It is the only solution.

Rhys Wardman (12)
Hipperholme & Lightcliffe High School, Lightcliffe

The Future

The world would be a better place,
If we all travelled at a slower pace.

We need to use our legs more and walk
And not drive round in fancy cars.

We need to not throw things away,
But recycle and use another day.

We could recycle our waste and sort things out
And not throw anything or everything out.

We need to keep our planet clean,
And not throw litter all over our streets.

It would be nice if people didn't smoke,
Then we could all breathe easier and not choke.

The world would be a better place,
If people could put a smile on their face.

Billy Thompson (11)
Hipperholme & Lightcliffe High School, Lightcliffe

Ain't No Game

Our world, it ain't no game,
Polluting is such a shame,
We can stop it,
But we have to try.

Poverty is so sad,
All the people with no mum or dad.
Sometimes no food to eat,
It is so sad,
But it's our world.

Chester Robinson (12)
Hipperholme & Lightcliffe High School, Lightcliffe

Untitled

Find a bin
And put your litter in
And save animals.

Walk instead of drive,
You will help oxygen survive.

Ice caps are melting,
So don't get a belting.

The monkeys scream,
The lumberjacks think they're supreme.
But they are making the world unclean.
So switch to energy saving lights,
It does not take knights.

Let's tell everyone around
What we have found.

Save your plastic and tins,
Before you put them in the bins.
Plant as many trees as you can,
Take time with your plan,

Before you get in your van.
Get out your bike and ride with all your might,
No need for cars,
It's easy to steer with your handlebars.

Robert Ainley (12)
Hipperholme & Lightcliffe High School, Lightcliffe

Recycle

Recycle, recycle, recycle your waste
Make the world a better place
Stop dropping litter, it is a disgrace
So help the climate change today
Recycle, recycle, recycle your waste
Thank you for making the world a better place.

Sasha Louise Dale (12)
Hipperholme & Lightcliffe High School, Lightcliffe

Lonely Crisp Packet

I live my life in the Co-op,
With all my other friends,
We will stick together
Until the very end.

But each and every one of us,
Know exactly where we are going,
We're going to get bought,
That's why we sing this poem.

Oh no, we shout as we are abducted from the rack,
Why does it have to be me, in my multipack.

I see my life float before my eyes
And hear a massive thump,
I've fallen, down , down, down,
Crushed in a big clump.

I'm rolling around like a child,
Doing cartwheels and making a racket.
This is me, it's who I am,
I'm the lonely crisp packet.

Laura Castle (11)
Hipperholme & Lightcliffe High School, Lightcliffe

Animals, Animals

Animals, animals, nearly all gone,
If we don't help them
There will be none.

Animals, animals, they're part of our lives,
If we're not careful,
They won't survive.

Animals, animals, they provide us with meat,
How nice they are
And also so sweet.

Sydney Stead (11)
Hipperholme & Lightcliffe High School, Lightcliffe

Pollution Is Not The Solution

Litter scattered on the ground,
Pollution spreading all around,
Global warming affects us all,
For everybody, small and tall.

Car-share, walking, clear skies,
Polar bears and penguins stay alive.

Trees dying,
Birds no longer flying,
Ozone layer tearing,
People no longer caring.

Car-share, walking, clear skies,
Polar bears and penguins stay alive.

It needs to stop,
Before the ice will drop.

No car-share,
No walking,
No clear skies,
Polar bears and penguins die!

Olivia Smith (11)
Hipperholme & Lightcliffe High School, Lightcliffe

Recycle Your Waste

Recycle, recycle, recycle your waste,
Make the world a better place.
Pick up your rubbish,
Don't be so mean,
Do the world a favour, why not go green?
Recycle, recycle, recycle your waste,
Make the world a better place.

Stevie Kennedy Reed (12)
Hipperholme & Lightcliffe High School, Lightcliffe

We Need It To Last

It's our world, we need it to last
When out in your car try not to blast
Try walking down your street
It's better for the Earth than driving your Jeep
Beep, beep
Take a quick shower rather than a bath
Save precious water, that's the right path
Let's all recycle and join the green scene
Come on, you know exactly what I mean
It's where all the coolest people hang out
It leaves the future of mankind in with a shout!

Faye Louise Cragon (12)
Hipperholme & Lightcliffe High School, Lightcliffe

The Black Rainforest

Here I stand, bright and tall, but sadly I'm in pain.
I'm wilting, I'm dying, because of acid rain.

The cheetahs growl, the monkeys scream,
The lumberjacks think they're supreme.

No oxygen to give, no carbon to live,
The world is dying too, because of CO_2.

I hear the saw, I feel the pain,
Here I go, I die again.

There are not enough trees in the world,
So you make a difference.

Andrew Rowley (11)
Hipperholme & Lightcliffe High School, Lightcliffe

Go Green

G reen leaves help us live, so don't chop down trees
O zone layer is falling apart, help it!

G o green, don't be mean.
R ead the news and stop abuse.
E very day we are destroying the Earth.
E veryone help the Earth survive.
N obody cares!

Matthew Crabtree (12)
Hipperholme & Lightcliffe High School, Lightcliffe

Threatening Waves

Waves racing,
Tsunami chasing,
Buildings falling,
This array of violence.

Rubble crushing,
Buildings demolished,
Fumes smelling
Of poisonous gases.

Rebuilding is the hardest part,
So let's crack on and make a start!

Kieran Rodger (12)
Hipperholme & Lightcliffe High School, Lightcliffe

Love For Animals

Don't be harsh, don't be mean.
We all care for you.
Take some time out for your animals.
Give them more treats and give them more food.
Give them more care that they need.
Save their habitat, now, before it's too late.

Romana Aziz (12)
Hipperholme & Lightcliffe High School, Lightcliffe

The Anxious Polar Bear

My friends are all around me,
And I'm rolling in the snow.
I see the ice is melting,
But no one wants to know.
My big, white, furry body
Is getting warmer too.
I need to share my knowledge,
But who will listen, who?

I'm not your average polar bear,
I know more than the rest,
Please invite me in
And treat me as a guest.
Then I will share my wisdom
With every one of you,
About humans wasting fuels
And causing CO_2.

Polar bears make footprints,
But not the carbon kind,
It's humans that don't have a clue
Of the mess they leave behind.
So every time you leave on
The computer, cooker or TV,
Think about this poem
And the sadness you leave me.

Olivia Burns (12)
Hipperholme & Lightcliffe High School, Lightcliffe

Recycle

R ecycle paper, plastic and glass.
E veryone can help to make the world last.
C lear the Earth, make it green.
Y ou can change it, don't be mean.
C are for the future,
L et's help.
E veryone - together can change climate change!

Lucy Grace Thackray (12)
Hipperholme & Lightcliffe High School, Lightcliffe

Recycling

Hey, hey, get out of bed,
Wipe your eyes you've got a busy day ahead.
Things to do, people to meet,
You've got rubbish around you're trying to beat.
Recycling makes the world clean
And it makes the grass and trees more green.
You can recycle glass, plastic and cans,
But it's hard work and you need a fan.
You could even give your old to a charity shop
And even receive a pink wooden mop.
Kids and adults can recycle
And you can recycle your old bicycle.
People really don't recycle much.
Look is that an old rabbit hutch?
Boxes and rubbish can be found in the dump,
Such as an old petrol pump.
Recycling you should do
And clean up all that yucky goo.
To help the country stay like this
We must do our little bit.
Recycling we have to do
And keep our country as good as new.
For when tourists come and look around
They have to see that we are proud.
If there weren't any recycling points
We wouldn't be able to flex our joints.
So come and help the world around
And see what can be found.
Cans, clothes, bottles, paper,
Do not wait until later.
Recycling is great, don't wait too late,
Don't delay, recycle today.

Ellie Charlotte Brook (12)
Honley High School, Honley

King Of Destruction

I love to change the world,
To cause storms and disasters.
I love the sight of litter,
Especially rubbish, and used plasters.

I hate the word recycle,
It doesn't kill the land.
I hate to reuse anything,
I think it should be banned.

I love to cost you money,
To buy unnecessary things.
I love to cut down rainforests,
And the destruction that it brings.

I hate the word recycle,
It should not be seen as clever.
I prefer to kill your future,
Life should not go on forever.

I love to cause pollution
And use up lots of fuel.
I love to destroy the landscape,
Cos humans are a fool.

I hate the word recycle,
Don't give it any thought.
You're taking away my game,
To wreck the world is my sport.

The King Of Destruction is my name,
To kill the planet is my aim.
To recycle anything is a shame,
And education kills my game.

Stephen Brown (13)
Honley High School, Honley

Recycling

Kicking cans on the street,
Litter on the ground,
Every single person you meet,
Look what you have found.

All it takes is a little time,
To pick up what you've thrown,
You don't want to get a fine,
So please try not to moan.

Put the bottles in your recycling bin,
Clear up all your waste,
Every little bit of tin,
Don't let me get on your case.

Leaving things on the floor,
Is not a good thing to do.
You will be getting a knock at your door,
As everyone else will too.

So if you're going to litter,
Think twice before you do it,
The world will be much better,
Without your waste added to it!

Claudia Kinghorn (11)
Honley High School, Honley

Animals

The more we kill, the more that go extinct.
They're there one minute, gone the next.
Why be so cruel, look at their conditions.

Why do this? Why be so selfish?
What have they done to us? Nothing.
Bang, they're gone.

Maariyah Ahmed (11)
Honley High School, Honley

Save Our Animals

S eries of animals
A lone and dying
V eering closer to death
E veryone needs to stop now or there will be nothing left.

O ctopus, sharks and fishes in the sea
U se the land for food
R e-evaluate what you have done

A ll the animals
N o care at all
I n years to come they will disappear
M aking all our lives a misery
A nswer all the questions about their struggle
L ife is what they need . . . and a little cuddle
S o *stop now!*

Brontë Roe (11)
Honley High School, Honley

Save The Sad, Sorry Animals

Save the animals
We all love them all
They haven't done wrong
Save them, they deserve it all

Why are they extinct?
What have they done?
Why extinct?
They don't deserve this to be done

Why, why, why?
What have they done?
Animals are fun.

Charley Bond (12)
Honley High School, Honley

Innocence Of Mind

Why do they do it?
What affects them?
Have they no conscience?
Do they not care?

People's lives,
Lived and lost,
What do they care?
Your fault if you're caught.

They call it a duty,
I call it a stain,
Upon the innocence ,
The petty innocence of our minds.

But how odd,
Our lives continue,
Despite these never perishing,
Never ceasing crimes.

It even has a name,
War,
It is not even considered a crime,
War.

Can I ask
When it will end?
Or is this crime to go on?
Not marred in its reputation and ways.
When will the guilty get their fair share
Of what the innocent have suffered?

Eleanor Antrobus (12)
Honley High School, Honley

The Ice Bear

The ice bear,
as white as snow,
as tall as a mountain.

Now lay dying in the melting snow,
starving.
The huge glacier that once stood proud and tall,
now lay dying in the snow.

Now a mere icicle,
he lay melting in the snow.
Drip, drop, drip, drop.

His limbs getting weaker,
and his aching, starving body
lying, dying in the snow.

'I wish I could die,'
the ice bear cried,
with a tear in his eye.
'Won't someone put me
out of my agony?'

But no one replied,
no one cared.
The ice bear lay, dying, in the snow.

So finally the ice bear
sleepily closed his eyes
for the last time,
then he fell into a deep sleep.
A sleep he would never awaken from.
The ice bear lies, dead, in the snow.

Taya Franco (11)
Honley High School, Honley

Pollution

What has happened to the world?
Creatures dying every day
Dolphins, sharks and tigers
Slowly dying in their own world

Sea water rising
Land getting flooded
More and more pollution
In this selfish world

Cars can run on petrol, diesel or anything else
But it won't help the environment
When they never walk
Get out the car and do something nice

The world is slowly dying
Animals are extinct
But people in the world
Can help if they try.

Ben Hudson (12)
Honley High School, Honley

Animals

A nimals dying every second
N ever going to end
I 'm trying to help people stop
M any people dumping rubbish on the floor
A nybody going to stop
L isten to me, please
S ome day there is going to be no animals left.

Sasha Clapham
Honley High School, Honley

Pooping Pollution

Pollution - stinky, horrible, bad.
A skidmark on the underpants of the Earth.
Rising sea levels,
Heating atmosphere.

Pollution - the dirty doings of humans,
A mighty sewer of the Earth.
The clouds of gross gas
Are killing the beautiful grass.

Pollution - humanity's disgrace.
They have destroyed all their grace.
Killing lots of life,
A knife of pollution.

Pollution - a massive bite,
We must fight
To find the light.
Then we'll be full of life.

Haydn Evans (12)
Honley High School, Honley

Tramp

H unting for money along the floor
O nly person sat there in the dark
M y house is a bench in the park
E ating whatever I can find
L east money in the world
E xtremely cold, laid tightly curled
S helter is my jumper keeping me dry
S adness and loneliness making me cry.

Jenna Comins (13)
Honley High School, Honley

Save The Animals

Save the animals
They are about to become extinct
Why do humans kill them?
We love them all

Why, why, why?
They haven't done anything
All they're doing is roaming free
Poor little things

Why, why, why?
What have they done to us?
Nothing
But we have done lots to them

Stop killing!
Save the animals!

Oliver Littleford (11)
Honley High School, Honley

Save The Environment

Don't go in your car
Walk very far
You will get fit
If you find an insect don't kill it

Save the universe
Save the Earth
Bring more birth
Don't be a curse

Don't sink
You should think
Then have a drink
Then you can blink.

Tuyab Chaudry
Honley High School, Honley

Recycle

Put it in the bin,
Don't commit a sin.
Put it in the bin,
Let the world win!

Don't litter the floor,
Just recycle.
It will be made into something new,
It's called the life cycle!

See people's litter on the floor,
Keep yours in your hand.
Wait until you arrive home,
In the bin it will land.

To stop the world getting polluted,
We must think of a plan.
So when you're walking down the street,
Keep your rubbish in your hand!

Jordan Walls (12)
Honley High School, Honley

Save Animals

S nakes slithering
A lligators swimming
V ipers hissing
E lephants eating

A lpacas spitting
N ewts splashing
I nvading aliens
M onkeys swinging
A lot of these animals need help
L et them live
S top polluting the Earth.

Rosie Benson (12)
Honley High School, Honley

Save The Environment

Why should the world have to cry,
'Help me, help me,
I don't want to die.'

Why does the land have to sink?
It happens quickly
Before we can blink.
Why does the planet suffer?
Why, oh why?
Global warming's getting tougher.

How can we help?
In lots of ways,
Do whatever this poem says.

Cut down on electricity,
Turn things off,
Have a quick shower
Instead of a long bath.

Cut down on water,
Turn taps off,
Recycle, reuse and . . .
Save the planet!

Sophie Burgess (11)
Honley High School, Honley

Save The Struggling Earth

The Earth is getting hotter
Why won't we think
To see what we can do
To save the struggling Earth?

Do something about it
Walk or bike to work
Just don't use the car too much
To save the struggling Earth

Why are we so lazy?
Turn everything off
To conserve our energy
To save the struggling Earth

Please stop polluting
Get it into your head
Don't ruin the environment
To save the struggling Earth

The Earth is dying
Like a person starving
It's so sick, so sad
We need to take action
To save the struggling Earth.

Daniel Wright (11)
Honley High School, Honley

Tax Wheeze

Global warming is a tax wheeze,
It will stay around until the government are pleased.
I'm sure Al Gore is a joke,
Talking of rouge poisonous smoke.

He told the polar bears twice
To go out and hide the ice.
Then all humans will believe
In my clever tax wheeze.

So if you feel out of pocket
And your tax has gone up like a rocket,
Blame the government who are pleased
In Al Gore's clever tax wheeze.

Harry Brook (13)
Honley High School, Honley

Earth

What will happen to the Earth?
What will we do?
How can we save ourselves?
Now look what we've done.

Cars, buses and trains,
All letting off steam,
Factories, ships
Puffing black gas.

We have killed them all,
Who will be next?
Animals, people,
The whole world?

Antonia Crookes (12)
Honley High School, Honley

War

All I can see is blood,
While I tramp across the mud,
Landed five hours ago
And in that time I have killed my bro'.
Minigun in hand
As I walk across the barren land,
Men falling beside me,
I really want to flee.
Dying men shouting for their mummy,
No one told me how awful this would be.
Here come the tanks
To shoot down our flanks.
Turning the ground to mud,
Their tracks covered in blood.
Here come the bullets,
Hitting men in their gullets.
One hits me in the heart
And with the world I part!

James Merewood (13)
Honley High School, Honley

Ice

I am a little polar bear
That has much care

I live on the ice
That used to be nice

The world around me is cold and snowy
The ice breaks every day
And water gets warmer day by day

There's less food to eat
And ice to see
I wonder what will happen to me?

Tia Hickson (14)
Honley High School, Honley

Animal Strike

Please help the world, it won't save itself.
Ocean animals dying, rotting in despair.
'Why are they doing this?' fish shout, 'It's unfair.
We're like a load of ornaments falling off the shelf.'

'I am Mr Badger, I am here to say,
You're destroying my house and you are gonna pay.
You should pay, it's brand new,
You ruined my kitchen and my loo.'

'Save my house, I'm really scared,
I have let off distress flares,
I want to get out of here,
My bones are weak and full of fear!'

Oliver Kirk (12)
Honley High School, Honley

The Neglected Cat

Large turquoise eyes shone
As the moonlight reflected,
Four silver paws strolled along the pathway
As the poor thing was neglected

Howls and lonely screams were passed through the wind
As tears of sadness dripped to the floor one by one
'Why?' it murmured, 'why?'
Who could have done this?
It would never be I
Such sad feelings and emotions
Which force you to cry.

Larissa Beaumont (11)
Honley High School, Honley

Bring Our Brave Brits Back

In Iraq no more death for oil
I hate it so much, it makes my blood boil
What's the point of WWII?
What's the point of WWI?
Maybe Ferdinand was killed
But now he's dead and gone
Hitler was a fool
Hitler had no heart
He probably had no idea in which destruction he'd take part
Saddam Hussein was a killer
He did all he could
He probably had an idea it would all end out in blood
Bush will soon no longer be president
Tell me why it is not over
The war in Iraq
Answer me this . . .
Why don't we bring our brave Brits back?

Louis Taithe (13)
Honley High School, Honley

The War

W   eeping families cry,
      as their children fight,
      some survive and some may die.

A nxious mums, dads, brothers and sisters
      wait to hear from their son, still alive,
      but others aren't so lucky,
      so families start to cry.

R unning backwards and forwards,
      gun in his hand, he fights for his country,
      but will he be left to stand?

Karlina Shaw (13)
Honley High School, Honley

Life

Sitting in my classroom
Wondering what to write
About global warming
That is such a fright.

Knowing one day
The Earth won't be the same,
The human race might cease to exist
Or take a new name.

The Earth is home
To many different creatures,
Not just to humans
But to animals, plants and beaches.

But, if your planet
Heats up much more
We and our surroundings
Fall down a trapdoor.

So let's try to keep
Our planet clean,
Free from dirt,
Let's all go green.

So try to recycle all that you can,
If we stick together
We'll succeed,
It's a good plan.

No one will lose out,
We will all gain,
From cleaning up the planet
From cleaning up our name.

Let's stop chopping down rainforests,
After all they're all our friends,
They change all the CO_2 we're producing
Into oxygen again.

Let's stop all the wars,
Because they're taking lives
And causing pollution,
We need to open our eyes.

Poverty is disgraceful,
There are just no words
For how we need to help
Those with no homes.

Racism makes me sick,
How people can discriminate
Against people just like themselves,
Only of a different race.

Littering is lazy,
Why not just find a bin?
Why instead, kill our planet
That everyone loves to live in?

So to finish off this poem
Listen to what I've said,
Remember, it is you who needs the Earth
To rest your head.

Rebecca Holloway (13)
Honley High School, Honley

Cut No Living Plant

Cut no living plant
No trees, no grass,
And move no rotting log.

Cut no living plant,
Nor rainforest or forest, no hedgerow
Cut no living plant
Nor sunflower
Nor bluebell
Nor daffodil
Or primrose.

So try your best,
Let nature do the rest
And cut no living plant.

Jason Taylor (14)
Honley High School, Honley

Will The World Ever End?

Homeless, unhappy, living on the street
No water, no food, no shoes on my feet
Cold, depressed, no cosy, warm home
No family or friends, I'm all alone.

I look around, I see poverty and war
I see different sorts of people, some rich, some poor
Some black, some white
In the big fight.

I see people that have lots of money
I try to have faith and try not to worry
I try to value what I have got
But what I've got is not a lot.

What can I do to make this world change?
There is no help that can be arranged
I always wonder if this world will ever end
But together we can help the environment, we can put it to mend.

Roya Nami (13)
Honley High School, Honley

The Turtle

The Galapagos turtle . . .
Her name should be Myrtle,
She is the last of her kind,
She's also very rare to find,
She's all alone,
No friends to phone,
She's 130 years old,
I'm surprised she hasn't grown mould,
She's locked in a zoo,
Kids see her and shout, 'Yoo hoo.'

Guy Smith (14)
Honley High School, Honley

Our World

Everyone wants to be more generous,
More thoughtful, more green.
But when it comes to money,
We are all less keen.
When there are so many mouths in the world to feed,
We do little to help, overpowered by greed.

This poem is about more than just one factor,
It's about war and poverty and natural disaster.
War and death and lack of medical supplies,
Would people care more if they were on the front line?

The rainforest, the jungle, such pressing topics.
Many animals live in the heart of the tropics.
Orang-utans and giant gorillas,
Hunted by poachers, like cold-blooded killers.

We should stop our world from becoming worse,
We should begin a new chapter,
A new sentence a new verse,
And release our lives from this morbid curse.

Edward Appleyard (13)
Honley High School, Honley

Racism - Victim

They call me names.
I can't join their games.
They call me black,
Then they give me a smack.

I feel like I want to die.
They spit in my eye.
They kick me in the face,
They hide my stuff all over the place.

I want to die.

Jack Williams (14)
Honley High School, Honley

Green Light

Follow the green light,
The light, the good,
Follow the green way,
You should, you should.

Recycle tin cans,
Glass bottles and such,
Newspapers and wrappers,
Thanks very much.

Turn down your heater,
Switch off your TV,
Turn off the light switch,
Will you help me?

Lower pollution,
Keep the air clean,
Lower the temperature
On the washing machine.

Global warming is bad,
Help us make it stop,
Doing this will help to make
The Earth's temperature drop.

Make sure you don't throw
Away plastic bags,
They don't decompose,
So the world will be glad.

Turn off plug sockets,
Reduce electricity
And the carbon footprint
That reflects each city.

Stop the greenhouse gases
Burning the ozone layer,
Help us to solve this case
So you can say . . .

I followed the green light,
The light, the good,
I followed the green light,
You should, you should.

Emma Sykes (14)
Honley High School, Honley

Save Our World

The world is dying
Caused by all the pollution
Give the Earth some hope

Lights are always on
TVs are always blaring
Switch them off standby

Washing machines hot
Just turn them down to thirty
Make the Earth cooler

Stop chopping down trees
Or have the animals gone
Forests are needed

Recycle tin cans
Use your plastic bags again
Change the world's future

Ice caps are melting
Temperature is changing
The world is dying

Help the world today
It won't change by tomorrow
Slowly but surely

This global warming
Is preventing our future
Do something right *now!*

Emily Rose (14)
Honley High School, Honley

Is It More Important

Is it more important,
For me and you as well,
To have new rollerblades,
Than for another girl who
Is my age and equal,
In Africa, where it is hot,
To have water, food, a home?

Is it more important,
For that girl down the street,
To get some more lipstick,
Than for a little one
So many miles away
In Africa, where it is hot,
To be safe, cared for and loved?

Those boys, playing football
On the green and safe field,
Don't stop to think of how,
Elsewhere, other boys kick stones
And must be glad at that,
In Africa, where it is hot,
Without grass, safety or shoes.

I'm not more important,
Nor is anyone who,
Has all the things they need,
Help them without water,
Protect them without homes,
In Africa, where it is hot
And people are important.

Rhiannon Rose Watson (14)
Kingstone School, Barnsley

The Copper Faces

There once lived copper-faces
In the forest, near our house.
With eyes like buttons on a suit,
Small, nimble as a mouse.
Their bellies were like leather,
Beaten hard and smooth and brown,
By years of aching sun,
The kind that comers with life off ground -
For they were never Earth creatures,
Destined for dusty trails,
Instead they sprang among the trees,
Arms spread, marmalade sails.
I'm sure I heard them in the night,
In some distant memory,
Their tiny squeaks replying to the creaks
Of my chair in the night-time breeze.
But that . . . oh that!
It is so very long ago by now
And rememb'ring them is a sign of age,
Sure as wrinkling on the brow!
For today the tiny copper-faces,
Today . . . well, they are gone.
Somehow the years slowly stole
The last traces of their song
And plucked their marmalade sails
From the sky between the trees.
Perhaps they sing to someone else . . .
But not to you or me.

Penny Cartwright (14)
Lawnswood School, Leeds

Untitled

As I walk down the road there is rubbish on the floor,
There are times we all think, *will they do it any more?*
There is a rubbish bin beside them
The rubbish bins don't excite them.

The street force help clean it,
We should help them do a bit.
They work day by day to keep the city clean,
They do everything for the Queen.

With all the rubbish they pick up
They recycle it and could make a plastic cup!

Reece Paulucy (14)
Myers Grove School, Sheffield

Energy

Coal was formed over 40 million years ago
Now it's almost gone
The cars and planes are using it all
Until there's nearly none
Factories are burning oil
Making loads of our power
That we are using every hour
We get the oil from the sea
And places like Iraq
But we are running out
And that's how it's going to be.

Daniel Smith (13)
Myers Grove School, Sheffield

War . . .

While the soldiers march towards their death,
As they march, their head held high,
Hoping they aren't going to die.
Their hearts pumping faster and faster,
Hoping their army won't be a disaster.

Training for years and years upon end,
Maybe for victory or just a short defend.
Holding on and holding on, trying to survive,
The other team are violent and alive.

Josh Harper (14)
Myers Grove School, Sheffield

Litter

People walking down the street
Dropping litter at their feet
It gets me mad when I don't see
People using the bins like me.

Some people ask 'What's a bin?'
It's the thing you throw your rubbish in
I'm too lazy, I can't win
I don't know how to use a bin.

Do your thing
And save the street
Use a bin
And make it neat.

Callum Reaney (14)
Myers Grove School, Sheffield

Bombs

As air-strikes light up the sky,
Innocent people begin to die.
Then all the survivors just ask, why?

They rode in with tanks,
Stole all our money from the banks,
We all huddled round in despair,
Then a plane came from nowhere
And blew the tanks with bombs in the air.

So why are we fighting
Or killing innocents?
They say they're stopping terror,
But I can still see villagers huddling round corners
And I can still see bombs everywhere.

Jack Phillips (14)
Myers Grove School, Sheffield

A Sloth's Plea

Z
Z
Z

I woke . . . to the sound of machines
Growling and snarling at me,
Two-legged creatures down on the ground
Carving and chopping down trees.

Their angry machines
And menacing glare
Taking our home,
They don't even care.

Where do they expect me
To live and go to sleep?
Where am I supposed to go
To curl up in a heap?

Why do you not understand
That these trees are our homes?
You cut them down and ship them off
But we can hardly moan.

The thing that really bugs me
Is that alive these trees help you.
They keep the world a greener place
And much more healthy too!

I know I'm not as big as you
And also not as strong,
But I have feelings just like you
And what you're doing is wrong.

Think about how you would feel
If all you had was lost,
No stability or safety
Now that's a pricey cost.

So now you know what happens
And how it affects me,
Please leave the trees alive and strong
So I can get some sleep.

Z
 Z
  Z

Hannah Moody (14)
Ryedale School, Nawton

Forests, Forests All Around

Forests, forests all around
Always standing still
Then men come and take some trees away
Forests, forests all around
They are getting less and less
Many years still to come
There may not be much left
Then a day, a very ordinary day
The weather starts to change
Black clouds start to come
Then a gush of rain all around
Then floods start to come
Forests, forests all around
Please come back and help
Come on trees
Suck up all the water
Clear the floods away
Forests, forests all around, we need you
Come back and help us please.

Christopher King (13)
St Pius X RC High School, Wath-upon-Dearne

Homeless

H ow do they survive?
O nly got the clothes on their back
M any of them sleep on the street
E very night
L ittle food to eat
E nergy gone
S ick of everything
S ometimes they feel suicidal.

Benn Dirienzo (14)
St Pius X RC High School, Wath-upon-Dearne

The Sea

What could that be floating around in the sea?
A carrier bag?
Maybe a bottle killing the fish, littering the shore?
Let the sea be how it was before!

Abbie Easton (12)
St Pius X RC High School, Wath-upon-Dearne

Homeless Poem

Homeless people scrounge in bins but rich people open tins
Homeless people beg for money, rich people find it funny.
Homeless people have no friends; rich people don't scrounge in bins.
Homeless people live on the street, rich people eat and eat.
Homeless people don't have jobs, rich people have pet dogs.
Homeless people go and pray, rich people have holidays in May.

Lewis Lynch (14)
St Pius X RC High School, Wath-upon-Dearne

Being Green

It's not easy being green
Rubbish everywhere you look
Pollution everywhere to be seen
Take a damn good look.

Pollution is filling up our atmosphere
It's spreading across the land
For all we know death could be near
Let's get this problem canned.

Poverty is uncalled for
In this day and age
Why do people have to suffer
Live life in a hungry cage?
It's not easy being green.

Lorenzo Camattari (14)
St Pius X RC High School, Wath-upon-Dearne

Never Forget!

Everyone should care
Never forget about the bins
That's very important.
In this world you need to help
Oh and recycle
Rubbish spoils the world
Never forget
Me and you should care and help
Everyone should care and help
Never forget
Take care of your world
Never . . . ever . . . forget!

Holly Sheridan (14)
St Pius X RC High School, Wath-upon-Dearne

Denial

I sit and listen
To the planes roar by,
And also the baby
Trying not to cry.
I'm out of the bunker
Looking at hell.
Wondering about
My water well.
Will it have survived like us?
Hooray! Happy day!
The war is over
At least for now,
But for the others . . .
Denial.

Daniel Chapman (14)
St Pius X RC High School, Wath-upon-Dearne

It's Good To Be Green

It's no good to be mean,
Please try to be green,
Put your rubbish in the bin,
Try to include all the tins.
Put things in the bin to help stop pollution,
Make a change, a new resolution.
It's cool to be green,
Not to be mean.
Recycle your litter,
Don't be bitter.
Look after your mountain range
You can stop climate change!

Lucy Staniforth (14)
St Pius X RC High School, Wath-upon-Dearne

Litter, Litter Everywhere

Litter, litter everywhere,
It's even at the fair!
Litter, litter everywhere,
It's even on the bus chair.
Litter, litter everywhere,
Don't just stand and stare.
Litter, litter everywhere,
Is it true you don't care?
Litter, litter everywhere
To make it stop we all must care.

Matthew Blakeley (14)
St Pius X RC High School, Wath-upon-Dearne

Green, Green, Green

Green, green, green, that is the theme
So save the world by keeping it clean.

Use the bins cos they are there
Save the world and show you care.

Recycling, recycling, that is green
Cos it's saving our planet by keeping it clean.

So help save our planet by going green
You know you can, don't be mean!

Georgina Brett (13)
St Pius X RC High School, Wath-upon-Dearne

Barnsley Rhyme

Pollution, pollution everywhere, world's falling apart
Cars, trains, lorries, they all let it art.
Unless summat's done, we won't be 'ere next year.
So let's hurry because before wi know it we'll all be livin' in fear.
Nar, it's time to settle darn, let's act quickly and keep a clean tarn.

Grace Ackroyd (14)
St Pius X RC High School, Wath-upon-Dearne

Rubbish, Rubbish Everywhere

Rubbish, rubbish everywhere
In the lift and on the stairs.
Rubbish, rubbish everywhere
Don't drop it even for a dare.
Rubbish, rubbish everywhere
Bin it if you care.
Rubbish, rubbish everywhere
Gather it all together and it's as big as a fair.
Rubbish, rubbish everywhere
Pick it up, do *your* share!

Oliver Ward (14)
St Pius X RC High School, Wath-upon-Dearne

Litter

Litter, litter everywhere
It is even on my chair!
Tidy, tidy, keep it tidy
Keep it clean on a Friday.
Litter, litter everywhere
Don't you even care?
Litter, litter everywhere
Don't you dare
Drop it anywhere
Except into a bin!

Alex Richardson (14)
St Pius X RC High School, Wath-upon-Dearne

War Is Bad

War, war is a horrible place
Fighting against the other race.
Why resort to violence to save face
Just end the disgrace - keep faith.

Dom Howell (13)
St Pius X RC High School, Wath-upon-Dearne

Changes

The sun was bright,
The sky was clear,
The water clean,
The grass green,
The world was warm,
The world was kind,
Everything's now changed
We're all to blame.

The sun is bright,
The sun is not,
The sun is melting,
The ice cap tops.
The polar bears with their gleaming fur
Treading through the snow unable to bear
Walking through, their journey so long
Yet they know they're nearly gone.

Abigail Cotton (14)
St Pius X RC High School, Wath-upon-Dearne

Pollution, Pollution Everywhere

Pollution, pollution everywhere,
It's making our oxygen dirty air.
Why is it that no one cares
That pollution, pollution is everywhere?
It comes from cars, it comes from stations
Even when we're on our PlayStations.
When you cook your Sunday meals
You're using our world's fossil fuels
So next time think about what you're doing
Before our world's an ancient ruin!

Bradley Peake (14)
St Pius X RC High School, Wath-upon-Dearne

Will It End?

Bombs and guns, death, despair
I'm sure there's peace over there.

Bullets breaking the speed of sound
With a thunderous blow they hit the ground.

I'm sure there's sunlight somewhere
Behind those dusty clouds up there.

Apache flying away up high
A missile flying through the sky.

Bombs exploding now and again
Then, through the air, fly valiant men.

Will this war ever end?
Maybe some day there'll be peace again.

Olivia Pratt (14) & Louis Staniforth (13)
St Pius X RC High School, Wath-upon-Dearne

The Beauty Of Nature

Please don't litter
It makes the world look bitter.
Be better every day
Making people come out to play.
Save the world
Save yourself
Just recycle
How hard is that?
Through the ages
The climate changes.
Save the energy
Don't waste it all,
Don't destroy the beauty of nature!

Andy Deng (12)
St Pius X RC High School, Wath-upon-Dearne

The Bitterness Of The Earth

The sun is getting hotter
The water level is getting lower
Food is getting short
The wars are becoming longer
The heat is getting higher
The storms are becoming thicker
Crooks are getting smarter
The weapons are becoming stronger
The people are getting worse
The waste is becoming more
The animals are becoming extinct
As society neglects and kills.
The weather is becoming different
As the waste is increasing
Soon trouble will follow as
Society starves itself to Hell.

Connor Patrick Hale (14)
St Pius X RC High School, Wath-upon-Dearne

Pollution

Pollution is very bad
It could make us all really sad.
It would change all the world if it could
Can we change it, yes we should!

It harms us in different ways
More and more as we count the days.
The wind sways up the trees
And we get more and more fees.

Matthew Burgin (13)
St Pius X RC High School, Wath-upon-Dearne

Litter

The world is full of it
So just use a bin
Litter is everywhere
Don't commit a sin.

You stand on it
See it on the streets
Just join us
At least try to be green.

It's cool being green
Let everything be clean
It's not easy being green
But try to clean up the scene.
So let's start, make a pledge from the hearts
To clean up our act, all be green
The world working together as a team.

Conor Cronly (14)
St Pius X RC High School, Wath-upon-Dearne

Saving The Environment

I saw a man throw something in the sea
What could it be?
It will harm the sea creatures
Destroying all of Earth's features.
We use cars too much
Let's walk and be more butch.
I think we should start to recycle
And start riding our bicycles.

Hayley Burke (11)
St Pius X RC High School, Wath-upon-Dearne

Saving The Planet

Finished with a packet,
Finished with a tin,
Don't put it on the ground,
Put it in the bin!

If you have a long bath,
Next day have a shower.
Don't have any more baths,
You're wasting eco power.

If you smoke for ages,
You're creating air pollution.
If you stop right now.
You *will* have the perfect solution.

Emily Hague (12)
St Pius X RC High School, Wath-upon-Dearne

Climate Change

The rain is falling from the sky
From the sky way, way, way up high.
Hitting the ground like a thousand pins,
In this state of weather, no one wins.
After a while the rain could gather
And destroy the world altogether.
People are running in devastation
This is caused by deforestation.
Now that was a poem about climate change
Just think that could happen to your nearest grange!

Lauren Poole (13)
St Pius X RC High School, Wath-upon-Dearne

A Solution To This Pollution

Too many cars roam the streets
Emitting too much pollution
We seriously need to find
A solution to his pollution.
We are too reliant
Why not buy a bike?
It might be something you like
We seriously need to find
A solution to his pollution
Or maybe do some walking
And bring a friend to do some talking.
We seriously need to find
A solution to this pollution.

Chad Bronson (14)
St Pius X RC High School, Wath-upon-Dearne

Discrimination Of The Soul

I sit here, the looming darkness surrounds me,
I am on my own, dead inside, kept alive by the pain inside.
I cannot hide; words are like bullets flying at my head,
In that case my body must be full of lead, sometimes I wish I were dead
For I cannot escape the continuous comments running round
in my head.
Why me, why me? I did not hurt them but I am nothing but scum
to them.
Day by day, it's like a needle tearing a hole in my soul,
I wish for death but death never comes.

John Shaw (13)
St Pius X RC High School, Wath-upon-Dearne

Litter

Litter, litter everywhere,
Why doesn't anyone in this world care?
All the bins on the street
Look at all the litter on that seat.
To work to help the environment,
Everyone should be intent.

Shannon Sarah Simpson (13)
St Pius X RC High School, Wath-upon-Dearne

Let's Make It Better

The world is becoming bare
Deforestation, CO_2 emissions
It's happening everywhere.
Making a hole in the ozone layer
No more food for the grizzly bear.
Racism, war, it's all the same game
Killing and fighting for one simple thing.
All this bullying for a big name
It's all wrong and we should be ashamed.

Hamza Nawaz (13)
Spen Valley Sports College, Liversedge

Animal Cruelty

Want to save our planet, forests and animals too?
Let them live the life they want to live.
We hear children pleading with their parents for pets,
I think, *what's the point, they won't look after them!*
Then we see homeless animals in the middle of nowhere
This is when the animals plead to be loved again,
Well, would you like to be that animal?

Kirsty Butterworth (13)
Spen Valley Sports College, Liversedge

Helpless Animals

Animals don't know any better
They need us to survive
If we all help to keep them alive
Rather than kill them
Help to heal them
Remember when you're being cruel
Animals have feelings too.

Samuel Humpleby (12)
Spen Valley Sports College, Liversedge

Animals

I am a sheep but I cannot sleep
Because of all the noises around the streets
And in the field I sit with my aching feet.
I am a cow so I now take a bow
I have fresh milk and my skin's as soft as silk.
I am a mouse I sneak around the house
Feed me please, my favourite's cheese.

Rebecca Todd (12)
Spen Valley Sports College, Liversedge

Why Ruin The World?

Animals, there are very many but in the next couple of years
There won't be hardly any if we don't recycle.
There will be corruption in the world,
Think of all these wild animals wanting to eat
But they can't eat because of the people that cause global warming.
Would you like this if it happened to you?
No, you wouldn't so please recycle for the good of the whole world.

Kristoffer John Parker (13)
Spen Valley Sports College, Liversedge

Me And My Tree

I am a monkey
I live in a tree
I'll have no home
If you kill my tree.

My tree is my home
I love it so much
Those men come and take it away
And now I have nowhere to stay.

If them men come
Us monkeys *will* die
So now I guess
We have to say bye-bye.

Leonie Jaye Horne (13)
Spen Valley Sports College, Liversedge

The War Must Stop

Running in, got my guns on ma back,
Get stuck in the war in Iraq.
Shot two guys, got me in the head,
Down ma mate got shot dead!
Run straight through, got a get away,
Got ta do, I got a live today.
Ma mate is gone, I'm feeling low,
Got to be brave, can't let it show.
We won the war, we got the throne,
Now we all just wanna go home.
So don't use guns, don't bomb that shop,
All the wars they all should stop!

Connor Ellis (13)
Spen Valley Sports College, Liversedge

The Green Poem

Be green
Turn off the machine.
Recycle
Ride your bicycle.
People living on the street
Give them money to make them eat.
Stop driving your car
That made you go far.
Walk instead
Get out of your bed.
People living on the street
Give them money to make them eat.
Send mail less
The possibilities are endless.

Avon Blyth (13)
Spen Valley Sports College, Liversedge

The Unnatural World

The natural world,
is unnatural to me.
Stumping and dumping,
it's now a rubbish heap.

The leaves on the trees
are now on the ground.
The birds' clapping beaks
are no longer around.

This season should be happy
so think clear and honest.
The animals need you
so save the rainforest!

Jennifer Newsome & Charlotte Day (13)
Spen Valley Sports College, Liversedge

Why?

Animals are dying all over the world
Cannot survive 'cause of our bad habits.
Polar bears dying, sloths too
Used for their furs to make money for you.
They collapse, they fall, they run, they walk
All for one thing, their life.
Cannot eat, cannot drink
Because of us stopping them think.
Stop these people, stop them now
How would you like it if I killed *you!*

Josh Cutler (13)
Spen Valley Sports College, Liversedge

Animals

Hit, punched and beaten,
Kicked out on the street,
No food, no water,
Just a painful death.
All they can do is walk away with eyes welling up.
Begging, whimpering, crying for forgiveness
Hearts broken, ripped in pieces.
Take them in, clean them up,
Save the life of a lonely pet.

Sarah Firth (13)
Spen Valley Sports College, Liversedge

World War, Peace

Yo, yo, ready for war but ready for peace,
Yo, hold tight in Iraq, just defend your back!
Just do what they did in World War II,
Play a bit of sport and make peace for you.
Save your battle for the Olympic Games
Even if it's in the rain.
And put whoever looses to shame
Because they're so lame.
Does not matter if you're black or white,
Don't be scared to go out at night
Because someone has to give you a fright
But whatever you do, *don't* fight!

Fraser Laycock (12)
Spen Valley Sports College, Liversedge

Help The Nation

Help, help, help,
Help the nation to recycle.
Use the amazing green bin,
Don't throw cardboard and plastic
Use the green box provided for you
This is for bottles and jars.
This world will be nasty
Let's change the way we live
Our children will grow up to a hell left by us
Time to make a change.

Elliott Hirst (13)
Spen Valley Sports College, Liversedge

Hearts Of The War

Boom! Boom! Boom!
The sound of war looms.
Bombs are dropped from enemy planes
But what, what will they gain?

Guns and knives
They will take people's lives.
Families ripped apart
Making holes in people's hearts.

Terrorists are homicidal
From despair people turn suicidal.
One day a few years ago, there's a day to remember
That fateful day on the eleventh of September.

Bombs attached to people's backs
Guilt is what those people lack.
Many people were dead and went up to Heaven
On that rotten day, July Seven.

Why, why, why
Do innocent people have to die?
Imagine children screaming,
Adults weeping.

Please no more war
No more, no more, no more!
Bring peace to the Earth
From the day you die since the day of your birth.

Charlotte Coates (13)
Spen Valley Sports College, Liversedge

What Matters

What does not matter, matters not,
Forgetting all that should not be forgotten.
Creatures all in time and space destroyed as we speak
A fallen egg, broken, returning not.
A free will? Far from it!

Jack Booker (12)
Spen Valley Sports College, Liversedge

Changing The World

Make our environment a happier place
Make peace with all the human race.
African, Asian, black and white,
Acquaint together without constant fight.

The climate, constantly changing,
Global warming, no hesitating.
Increasing carbon footprint,
Can't you take a hint?

No one wants to find a bin
Just look around then put your litter in.
People want their rubbish bins empty
'Cause now there is increasingly plenty.

All around the world poverty stands
Thirsty, cold, hungry hands.
No longer will it remain a mystery
Can you help make poverty history?

Homeless people cold and wet,
Turn to the streets, could be in debt.
Damp and forgotten, dark alleyways
Depressed and careless see it every day.

Chloé McMullan (13)
Swinton Community School, Mexborough

War

People dying in war zones
Lying on other's bones.
People don't respect the dead
Who lie in their bed - RIP.
Ones who saved the world
While people are safe in their beds curled up.
People don't respect the dead
Who lie in their bed - RIP.

Cole Tolley (13)
Swinton Community School, Mexborough

Black Or White

Black or white
Dark or light,
Should we question people's race
Because of the colour of their face?
Should we always really fight
Over people black or white?
There are always big debates
Over what race people hate.
Does it matter what's on the outside?
Because we are all the same on the inside.
The world would be a better place
If we learnt to respect each other's race.

Luke Allen (13)
Swinton Community School, Mexborough

Recycle

R ecycle
E ndless possibilities
C ars can become flares
Y ou can make a difference
C ut down on pollution
L ong stretches of wasteland can disappear
E veryone can help.

Jessica Rowley (13)
Swinton Community School, Mexborough

Being Green

Burning buildings, dying people
Animals' extinction, what did they ever do?
Stop polluting, make the difference
It could all be thanks to you.

Millie Clamp (12)
Swinton Community School, Mexborough

Global Warming

Global warming, global warming,
Climate change, climate change,
If we don't stop polluting,
If we don't stop polluting,
We will die, we will die!

The facts are true
And will affect you.
Wherever you run,
Wherever you hide.

Global warming, global warming,
Climate change, climate change
If we don't stop polluting,
If we don't stop polluting
We will die, we will die!

We must change
Or we will be in danger.
All these things we need to do
And some day you will need to too!

Samuel Bennett (12)
Swinton Community School, Mexborough

Pollution

P oisonous gases
O ver our nation
L ook around you
L ike what you're seeing
U nwanted gas pouring from buildings
T he world will burn up and die
I f you don't stop it
O verhead the sky is dying
N o, I don't like what I'm seeing!

Lewis Creamer (13)
Swinton Community School, Mexborough

War!

Some people think war is crude
Others think it's fun
Countries fighting to see who wins
With pistols, rifles and submachine guns.
Wars can start at any point
The sixties, the nineties, even now.
The soldiers always try their best
To not let their country down.
But they need strategy and orders of what to do
To attack or to break their opponents defences,
They obey the orders and the fight continues.
All wars must come to an end
It can last for four, five, seven years
But when the war has ended
We are *all* left in tears.

Thomas Drew (12)
Swinton Community School, Mexborough

Sgt Mjr Gelder

Here I am in Iraq
Our English soldiers, under attack
I'm in my kit from the TA
Dreading every single day.
A bomb goes off, another friend dies
While back at home the Government lies.
We need your support, we fight for you!
I mean, is that the best you can do?
I haven't showered in a fortnight
In my bed, an explosion, I shudder with fright
I eat a carrot, my meal for today
Each night I wish and I pray.
Like a robot's programmed to do
I fight for my country and I fight for you!

Paige Gelder (13)
Swinton Community School, Mexborough

How To Help Stop Pollution

Now here's a solution
To help stop pollution,
Lately there have been large floods
Far too big for any sized hoods.
Don't be bitter,
Bin your litter.
Please don't make another war
Or the world will become more poor.
Save the paper will you please
So that we can help the trees.
To stop melting the polar ice caps
Can you *please* turn off your taps.
So there you go, please don't hesitate
Or it will be far too late.

Lauren Cooper (12)
Swinton Community School, Mexborough

The Rainforest

Deep in the forest the tigers lay
And the colourful canaries flutter and play.
Swooping and jumping from tree to tree
The monkeys love to be so free.
The only noise that could be heard
Was the swooshing of wings from a courageous bird.
Then in the next instance
Was a sound far in the distance,
It was coming closer from the front, back and side,
The animals panicked and ran to hide.
As the trees now fell to their fate
The animals watched in pure hate.
Their habitats have now gone
And the animals have had to move along.

Sophie Barnett (13)
Swinton Community School, Mexborough

Homelessness

H undreds of people living on streets
O nly a blanket to keep them warm
M any people will throw me a penny
E ven that won't buy me a meal
L onely children kicked out from their homes
E ndless comments they get from others
S ome on their own, some with brothers
S cared and frightened
N o one to love them, no one to care
E very day it gets worse, it's just not fair
S melling like a dustbin, there's no shower out here
S itting alone and living in fear.

Zoe Brain (13)
Swinton Community School, Mexborough

War

People of the world, the horror of war
It's like being mauled by big sharp claws
The horrible war it's really a dread
The enemy won't stop till most are dead.

Out in the open given the order to hold
Out in the freezing all frosty and cold.
This is evil just over the top
I'm saying this out loud, 'This must stop!'

Joshua Bell (12)
Swinton Community School, Mexborough

On The Streets

On the streets
In the gutter
With nothing to eat
Not a sound or mutter
In the dark
All alone
Only a bark
From a cosy home.
Strangers passing by
Drunk out of their head
I don't want to cry
I just wish I was dead.

Yeorgia Argirou (12)
Swinton Community School, Mexborough

Recycling

R ecycling makes a better place
E nvironments will blossom
C lean up after yourself
Y our help is vital
C ans and bottles need to be recycled
L itter is unhygienic
I magine what your help can do
N o more waste on the streets
G reat things can be accomplished by recycling.

Christopher Birks (13)
Swinton Community School, Mexborough

Save The World

Live in a clean and healthy place
You can save the human race
If you throw your rubbish in the bin
You'll never regret anything.
Bring the world to reunite
All colours black and white
Just make the world a better place
And you'll have a smile on your face.
Climate is constantly changing
Carbon footprint and global warming.
When the skies are grey and blue
What can you really do?
Homeless people on the street
Cold and wet with nothing to eat.
All alone with no money to spare
All they want is love and care.
Make love not war
Acquaint together, fight no more.
All countries have their right
But still we can reunite.

Hannah Roebuck (13)
Swinton Community School, Mexborough

Peter The Tiger

Flesh-eater named Peter
A hunter to the end
Always happy, always relaxed
Never sad, never bad
A tongue so licky, never picky
A tail that flicks as he sits
Always here, always there
Never stopping to give a care
Let's hope he roams his domain forever
Don't let him disappear.

Bradley-Allen Sharp (13)
Swinton Community School, Mexborough

Litter

Mucky litter all around, smelly litter on the ground
Move this litter and you'll be saved, a brighter future you will crave.
This set of instructions are all so easy, follow them
and this world won't be cheesy.
Pick it up and go to a bin, bend over then put it in.
Make this world a better place because *you* can save the human race.
Little children drop litter, them brats, carry on and you'll attract rats!
Save this world, pick up rubbish.

Katie Parkin (12)
Swinton Community School, Mexborough

Making It A Better Place

Pollution, it is so gruesome,
Power stations, they're taking over the nations.
Don't throw it in the bin, that's a bore,
And also don't throw it on the floor.
Pop down to the recycling bin and put it in there instead.
War, what the heck's it for?
We don't need it, there's people living in pits, what's it for?
Make it a better place and it will put a smile on your face.

Ben Liddle (12)
The King's School, Pontefract

Climate Change

Climate change, climate change
We all should be ashamed.
Global warming, global warming
It comes without warning.
The planet heating up and up
So we need to step up
Go do your bit!

Heather Tonks (13)
The King's School, Pontefract

Litter

Smells overhead are bitter
The street's covered with litter
Litter dropped every day
Does it have to be that way?
We believe one day we'll see
A world clean and shiny
That is why we say
Our brushes will sweep the litter
Our mops will clean the street
Even if you don't want to, we do!
Gooey food on the floor
Chips dumped near people's door
Cans of Coke makes cats choke!
Crisp packets cause rackets
We have a solution to stop street pollution
It's big, the thing is a bin!

Lucy Hill (12)
The King's School, Pontefract

The Four Rs

Stop throwing litter on the ground
Use a bin that can be found.
Reuse, reduce, recycle and repair.

Old clothes now out of fashion
Recycle into something with a passion.
Reuse, reduce, recycle and repair.

Take plastic bottles to the recycle tip
You never know it could become a ship.
Reuse, reduce, recycle and repair.

Reduce the amount of household waste you make
Remember the four Rs for goodness sake!
Reuse, reduce, recycle and repair.

Olivia Mountain (13)
The King's School, Pontefract

Save The World

Lower the volume
Switch off that light
Don't waste electricity
An eco-world is in sight.

A world of all religions
A world of all colours
There's no room for racism
Or bullying for that matter.
Save the rainforest
Save the nature of all to see
Soon it will be gone
'Help us,' we plea.

So let the world be a better place
Full of love and kindness.
It's a way we will love the world
And love is something priceless.

Kate Maeer (13)
The King's School, Pontefract

Pollution

I woke up in the morning
When the day was dawning
I got in the car,
I didn't go far.
I could have walked
I'm such a fool
With my friends I could have talked
On the way to my high school
But when I got there
I couldn't help but stare
Everyone was making
Pollution in the air!

Ryan Kaye (12)
The King's School, Pontefract

Save The World

Turn the telly off
Walk to school
Shut down the computer
And turn the tap off too.

End the wars
Pick up your litter
So the environment
Doesn't get bitter.

All those things
Can help the globe
But to do it
We have to devote
Our trust and care
Into nature
To help us save
The world.

Jack Hiorns (11)
The King's School, Pontefract

Be Green

Some people start destruction
Others start material reduction.
Some people recycle and reuse
Others think it's stupid and refuse.
Some leave the chewing gum on the floor
Others start a nuclear war.
Someone starves and another one suffers
And some just don't think of others.
Some people think it's hip to be green
And those that don't aren't real human beings.

Isobel Bonnefoy-Jenkinson (12)
The King's School, Pontefract

War

War, what is it really?
Do we need it?
What does it do?
It doesn't solve or protect
Or save lives, it takes them
In the most vicious way possible.

War, it causes argument.
It causes pain.
It causes suffering.
It causes hate.
It replaces friendship.
It replaces love.
It replaces what we're supposed to be fighting for.

War, it makes us forget
What we're fighting for.
Forces innocent people
To fight to keep it alive.
It thrives on hatred and death.
It cheers when it starts
It's the disease we can't be made immune to.

Naomi Jones (13)
The King's School, Pontefract

Recycle Rubbish

R ubbish and packets all over the floor
E verywhere I look there is more and more
C hildren playing out on the dirty street
Y ou can see all the rubbish around their feet
C ardboard boxes, newspapers too
L ots of them together will be made to be new
E veryone should always put their rubbish in the bin or recycle!

Kelsey Mansell (12)
The King's School, Pontefract

Why?

Why does the fish swim on his back
Belly on show, eyes looking black?
Why he's not swimming, he is dead!
Pollution in the river, he's been fed.
Animals in zoos, nowhere to roam,
Why have we humans stolen their home?
Rainforests cut down just for wood,
Would we stop this if we could?
The ozone's got holes in, this we know,
The ice caps melting, so is the snow.
Drive your cars and pump the gas,
The whole world's doing it on mass.
Turn up the heat and make your home hot
We can't see the damage so why not?
The Earth itself is warning us all
Make some changes or suffer the fall.
Why have we treated this world we live on
With such disrespect, soon all will be gone.
We must change our ways and learn form the past
It's the only way as a race we will last.
Look after ourselves and the planet too
Why wouldn't you?

Alix Edwards (12)
The King's School, Pontefract

Earth

The rainforests here are being cut
The pollution is clogging my gut.
Put waste in a bin
Fight for recycling
And reduce our carbon output.

Ryan Bellas (12)
The King's School, Pontefract

These Are The Rules Of Recycling Things

*(This is sung to the theme of 'These are a few of my favourite things'
by Julie Andrews in 'The Sound of Music')*

Recycle your trash
Keep your streets nice and clean
Pick up your rubbish
So streets shine and gleam
Sort out your garbage
In different bins
These are the rules of recycling things.

Recycle your junk
Say no to litter
Cos the world's a mess
Simply remember to pick up your trash
And then the world is
Cleaner!

Bethany Lamb (12)
The King's School, Pontefract

Save The Environment

I hear the sound of car brakes screeching to a halt.
I can see litter covering the streets like an icy blanket of danger.
I smell exhaust pipes polluting the air.
I feel the heat of the burning sun heaving down on my shoulders.
I taste smoke!

Chelsea Thomas (12)
The King's School, Pontefract

Night-Time Warning

You'll never guess what happened
Asleep in bed last night
I fell through a hole to a far-off land
In a flash of blinding light.

Arriving there I was greeted
By a bunny ten-feet high
'You're destroying planet Earth,' he said
'With pollution in the sky.'

'I must point out you're wrong,' I said
'Admit it that you lie.
I turn off taps, I switch off lights
Destroying Earth, not I!'

But Bunny said, 'You still use cars
When travelling to school
You don't recycle anything
Don't play me for a fool!'

Then I awoke with breakneck speed
And sat up bolt upright,
His words had hit me hard and fast
And given me a fright.

I've made a resolution,
I'm going to start anew.
I'll be a greener person
And you can be one too.

Recycle all your rubbish
And do not use the car.
Turn off lights and planet Earth
Will be a better place by far.

Elise Groves (12)
The King's School, Pontefract

Atmospheric Frustration

We need your motivation
This poem's for your education
We need to save the nation
From atmospheric frustration.

We are in desperation
From the overcrowded population
So listen to this information
It's our planet's compilation
We need to stop deforestation
And stop rainforest deprivation.

Halt animal extinction
With absolute distinction
Reduce your illumination
And decrease CO_2 pollution.

There's not an explanation
For positive climate change correlation
Now that's good alliteration
But let's talk discrimination
There ain't no fascination
In causing aggravation.

You don't have an invitation
To plan a war operation
I have made an observation
Homelessness is in gestation.

I know you have temptation
But use your imagination
And reduce complication
For our next generation
So let's start this revolution
And take these points into realisation.

Melissa-Jayne Godfrey (12)
The King's School, Pontefract

I Dream Of A World

I dream of a world
Where the air is pure and clean.
I dream of a world
Where the thought of poverty is obscene.

I dream of a world
Where the world is united in peace.
I dream of a world
Where the living do not suffer the deceased.

I dream of a world
Where automation gives way to nature.
I dream of a world
Where we do not put the Earth through torture.

I dream of a world
Where trees do not fall to iron-toothed machines.
I dream of a world
Where trees and nature are first before our own means.

I dream of a world
Where extinction is history.
I dream of a world
Where the word homeless is a mystery.

I dream of a world
From the cold ground in night.
I dream of a world
Where my dream will become reality with all my might.

Please help these dreams come true.

Christian Smith (12)
The Mirfield Free Grammar School, Mirfield

A World Of Racism

There's a whole lot of world
Half black and half white
Though people get picked on
They may even fight.

No matter what colour
We are just the same
No matter what size
No one is lame.

What's on the inside
Should count the most
No matter what country
Beijing or the coast.

So put a stop to racism
That's what counts
Do it now
Before the trouble mounts.

Charlene-Melissa Clarke (13)
The Mirfield Free Grammar School, Mirfield

A Better World

Lots of people in one spherical world
Why do people have to judge the races?
Of the people, lots of insults being hurled
Just because of different coloured faces.

We are all the same in every way
In our world there are many different places
Each person has a different coloured face
Each of them are different, that's all I've got to say.
A little black boy, cold and lonely
The little black boy pushed out of the way
He's all alone from night to day
Because of the colour of his skin
If the racism doesn't stop, who knows, if only
This world could end, yes, it could blow!

Amy Curtis (13)
The Mirfield Free Grammar School, Mirfield

Blue Bin Day

On blue bin day
The dustbin men take my bin away
Badum, badum, badum!

They attach it to the back of the truck
Where the machine lifts it up
Kerching, chang, ching!

The hungry lorry gobbles it all
In his throat it begins to fall
Munch, crash, crunch!

The big tall lorry drives away
Leaving me waiting for the next blue bin day, yeah!
Beep, beep, beep, recycle on your blue bin day!

Ashley Norris & Jacob Webster (13)
The Read School, Selby

Poaching

I hope I can't be seen,
This man is very mean.
I hope I don't get shot,
Will I die or not?

I hope my life won't change,
I feel so very strange.
I want to be here a little bit more
Before he breaks me down to the core.

I can hear his breath behind me,
Please just leave me be.
Why am I the one?
I've never done anything wrong
Could this be the end of my life?

Luke Derbyshire (11)
The Read School, Selby

War Is A Horrible Time

War is a horrible time
It's almost the worst crime.
Bash, bang, bing, boom!
The bomb destroyed another room
As the war goes on and on.
More and more lives are gone.
As the planes are always flying
The babies are always crying.
The deaths are growing
And the blood keeps flowing.
The soldiers work day and night
In the morning there's a sense of fright.
War is a horrible time
It's the worst crime.
Why do you fight?
It just isn't right!

Kashir Nair & Danny Spinks (13)
The Read School, Selby

Rainforest

R ainforest as pretty as a necklace
A ll is peaceful
I t's so calm you can fall asleep relaxed
N o noises apart from animals moving
F orever peaceful until
O h gosh, they come, the evil ones!
R ushing about the machines start to chop
E veryone stops, one more tree is left
S ilence then suddenly
T imber! The rainforest is ruined.

Jenny Rockliff (13)
The Read School, Selby

Pollution

Pollution, pollution
Do you have a solution?

A whisper of wind
In the sky
I hate your animals
I will make them die.

Whilst you're snoozing
I am oozing.

I smell of rotten meat
And stinky feet.

The stench is so bad
I'll make you star-crazy mad.

I am a big green killing machine.

I'm as green as a boggy
I'm an old foggy.

There's only one solution
To solve this pollution.
Don't drive to school
Ride a bike
Or go on a ginormous hike.
Pollution, pollution
We have a solution.

Megan Wilkinson, Megan White & Jacob Taylor (14)
The Read School, Selby

Global Warming

Ice caps melting
Temperatures rising
Disasters happening
It must be global warming!

Sea levels increasing
Ozone layer widening
Disasters happening
It must be global warming!

Cliff walls eroding
Smog levels increasing
Disasters happening
It must be global warming!

Rainforests falling
Rubbish levels mounting
Disasters happening
It must be global warming!

Wind farms in operation
Solar power a possibility
Disasters happening
It must be global warming!

It's not too late
So don't hesitate
Disasters happening
It must be us!

Harry Torn (12)
The Read School, Selby

My Poem

Wind, blow me away
In a bin I go
Won't be allowed out till I go
To the tip; that's the place
Litter loves to go.

The bins are the place
That litter hates
It hides in alleyways and under cars
Just to get away from the bins.

Makes the world a muckier place
The place we live is such a disgrace
So clean up
And make your world a cleaner place!

Tom Birdsall (12)
The Read School, Selby

Rainforests

Rainforests are our friends
So why do we go 'n' chop 'em down
Habitats lost for just no reason
Animals dying cos of our greed
So let us stop when there's just no point
When we build we're tearin' down
The house of that poor little bird
It's not just birds, there are tigers too
And there are lots of others we need to save
So recycle your paper!

James Welsh (13) & Albert Barber (12)
The Read School, Selby

War

War is the word I hate
People are sent out to fight, there is no debate.

Most people don't want to go
But that leaves people feeling low.

When people cry it's very sad
And that leaves people feeling distressed and mad.

Think about children, we're only small
And leave our fathers standing tall.

We want our dads there to watch us grow
Form shoulder to shoulder and head to toe.

If your dad's a soldier you need to know
If he didn't like it, he wouldn't go!

Molly Fidler (12)
The Read School, Selby

Dolphins

Dolphins, dolphins, glamorous girls
Shining in the sea like a pearl.
Dolphins, dolphins what can you see?
They are pretty princesses in the sea.
Dolphins, dolphins, splashing around,
Till the sun goes down, down, down.
Dolphins, dolphins always fighting,
But they are fast like lightning.
Dolphins, dolphins getting caught
But all they want to do is be free.

Annabel Lambeth (13) & Megan Rhodes (14)
The Read School, Selby

Penguins

Penguins are like fish
No penguins would be like no sweets
Crunch, crunch, crunch!
As they are walking in the snow
Crunch, crunch, crunch
Splash, splash, splash!
As they jump into the sea.
Splash, splash, splash!
Penguins are like the kings of the sea
People need penguins
A penguin is as tall as a human
So don't attack them
They might attack back.

Danielle Marritt & Angel Wu (13)
The Read School, Selby

The Big Green Poetry Machine

Help, please help the endangered animals
Tigers, monkeys, elephants, pandas and lots more
Tiger, tiger - a cat family
The tiger; extremely proud of its territory
Recognised by its fur
Tigers normally live for ten to fifteen years,
That is a tiger.
Panda lives alone
Panda weights three-hundred pounds
They can be fierce and that's black and white pandas.
They all are endangered animals and they all live for different years
They are all different.

Kajin Osman (13)
Winterhill School, Kimberworth

The Tigers

Tigers, tigers around me,
Yellow, orange, black they can be.
Graceful beauty there's no doubt
The stripes, the lean lines they cut out.
A figure swift, a figure fast
An animal that's cool to the last.
As keen as cunning fills their eyes
They'll pounce, attack with sole surprise.
Falling on their startled prey
With all the horror they can slay.
Scratches on your arms, your wrist
You're hurting badly, lies their kiss.
By magnificent and surely might
They're keen they're cunning
They snarl and fight.

Leanne Denman (12)
Winterhill School, Kimberworth

The Shark

A dangerous predator, its name is the shark,
It swims around constantly hunting in the dark.
One bite is all it takes for the oceans to turn red,
You feel a pain throughout your body and before you know it
                                        you're dead!
Blood is in the water, blood is everywhere,
Then the monster looks at you with its empty stare.
But before you think that this creature lives to eat and slaughter,
Just remember it will soon be extinct, that majestic fin in the water.

Conor Allen-Roberts (13)
Winterhill School, Kimberworth

Imagine It Green!

Become green, don't be mean!
Be kind, use your mind.
See what you can do
To keep the skies blue
To keep the air clean.
Recycle, reuse, reduce.
Deer, lions, bear and giraffe and moose
You name it
At this rate they won't be around much longer,
So let's save them!
Pollution, extinction, it's gonna happen
One day to stop it altogether we can find a way
It's spreading fast and once it's here at last
The world won't be a happy place
So us as the human race
Must be green.

Danielle Littlewood (13)
Winterhill School, Kimberworth

Bullying

Why bully people, what's the point?
People are getting hurt every single day because of bullying.
Some people get bullied because of their weight,
Think about it, what would you do if it was you?
Bullying has got to stop before something horrible happens.
What if it was you getting bullied, how would you feel?
Sad, hurt, lonely and think about other people,
It has got to end, there is no point in bullying people, it's *not* cool,
It's being mean to someone and is horrible.
Racism! A form of bullying,
Black or white we are all human.
People should be treated the same whatever colour skin they have got,
We are all one.

Karryn Zambe (11)
Winterhill School, Kimberworth

The Tiger

T igers' stripes are like flashes of orange lightning
I ts menacingly fierce teeth grip its prey and draws blood
G iven the chance he will grab anything
E very night they will sleep, peacefully silent and still
R eally endangered, hunted for their beautiful fur
S ave them, stop hunting, save the world.

Annabel Drakeford (13)
Winterhill School, Kimberworth

Dolphins

D olphins are cute
O ceans are polluted
L ives in the sea
P layful like a puppy
H appy most of the time
I ndigo and sometimes blue
N owadays dolphins are protected by laws
S pecies of dolphins are rare, please save the dolphins.

Mariam Hussain (12)
Winterhill School, Kimberworth

The Bad Lad

Bullying is bad, go tell your dad you're not a bad lad .
When you get hit don't have a fit
You're not a bad lad, you're not cool, you're a big fool!
If it goes wrong always hold your tongue
Don't answer back, you'll get a crack!

Oscar Chadwick (12)
Winterhill School, Kimberworth

Bullying

We're all the same on planet Earth
Bullying really is lame
So come on everybody, let's put these bullies to shame
You see them in the park acting smart
You better watch this nasty lark
You told me I wasn't cool
You told me I was a fool
I see people walking round town
Always getting people down
Why do such a thing?
Who invented bullying
Some people take it too far
By pushing the victim in front of a car!

Samantha Shirtliffe (12)
Winterhill School, Kimberworth

Make It Stop

Some people think bullying is fun
Those people are sad and dumb.
They don't care about how I feel
But if it was them, they would squeal.

Those people make my life sad
They wind me up until I go mad.
I feel so alone and cramped in
But there is a way to win.

There's a way to stop it if we work together
If we worked hard we can stop it forever.
Now it's stopped I feel so free
Ever since then they never teased me.

Olivia Abell (12)
Winterhill School, Kimberworth

Bullying

I'm the one you pushed and shoved.
I'm the one you never loved.
I'm the one you always teased.
I'm the one who could never please.
I'm the one who you made cry.
I'm the one who wanted to die.
The teacher came to see what was wrong,
I told her everything and mentioned your name.
It's not me you should shout at, you're the one to blame.
Everything started to go right, I even got a friend
Then all of a sudden before I knew, I became popular just like you!

Abbie-Leigh Gostling (12)
Winterhill School, Kimberworth

Bullying

Don't bully, it's not right either black or white.
Don't bully, it's not fun; the fight could include your daughter or son.
Why does size matter, it shouldn't do, don't bully or you could
get back kung fu!
Jack is Jack, Sue is Sue, that is their names, not boff or goth.
So just remember two tiny words, it goes like this
Don't bully!

Jade Marshall (12)
Winterhill School, Kimberworth

The Tiger

T iger
I n the dark jungle
G rowling and waiting for its prey
E ven in the blistering heat
R ed-hot heat from the sun will not stop this tiger from getting its prey.

Alex Barker (13)
Winterhill School, Kimberworth

Become Greener

The world is no greener
People are meaner
Animals are dying
Aeroplanes are flying
Pollution is spreading
The animals are dreading
Extinction they fear
So save the deer
Recycle your paper
Help the forests keep animals safer
Do all you can
To help them have a long lifespan
Extinction is bad
So help stop it before things get mad
It's happening *now!*

Danielle James (12)
Winterhill School, Kimberworth

The Wonderful Tiger

If to see a world without thee
This world would be a disgrace
Knowing we didn't save this wonderful place.

I live in fear
Not knowing if they're here or near.
They hurt me for my fur
But I scare them away with my purr.
Cute and cuddly, scary and nasty,
They won't catch me because I'm ready and wanting to last
As I am the tiger!

Kieran Paul Ward (13)
Winterhill School, Kimberworth

Bullies Are Mean

Bullies are mean
Bullies are mad
Bullies are cruel
But in fact, they're very sad.

Bullies are dangerous
Bullies are scary
Bullies are fierce
And bullies are just like fairies.

Bullies are stupid
Bullies say they'll bounce you like a bunny
Bullies are silly
And they're not even funny.

Thomas Hill (12)
Winterhill School, Kimberworth

Different But Good

White, tanned, brown, black
Colours of your skin
So don't turn back
And be happy what you're in.

People that bully you
Should be banned
They all said, 'Boo!'
So I can't put up my hand.

I told someone once and for all
Now I am happy
And I stand tall
So all be happy with me.

Jessica Smales (12)
Winterhill School, Kimberworth

Help Be Greener!

Recycle your paper
So the animals are safer
Help the world become greener
And the skies cleaner
Pollution is spreading
The animals are dreading
The short life they live
Much more we should give.
Thank you.

Rachel Haywood (12)
Winterhill School, Kimberworth

Bullying Poem

Big or small, bullying will get you nowhere
You'll always be the same if you don't act now
Life is too short
Like everybody we're all the same
You will not get far from bullying
I want you to leave me alone
Never let bullies get you
Go away bullies, we don't like you!

Hansa Sajaad (12)
Winterhill School, Kimberworth

What's The Point?

I used to be bullied now I'm not
I told a teacher and it stopped!
They called me names about my skin
At first I was too tall now I'm too thin.
They thought it was cool,
I looked like a fool.
I'm so happy, I'm so glad,
That it's all gone away, I'm no longer sad.

Hannah Williams (12)
Winterhill School, Kimberworth

Racism

I look here, you look there, what do you see?
Racism!
I look here, you look there, what do you see?
Black and white playing together.
Let's stop racism, it's not right
Because you're black or white.
Don't fight or punch or kick or bite,
Be nice, they're just like you
Let's stop racism together, woo!

Samuel Hirst (11)
Winterhill School, Kimberworth

Black Or White!

Black or white, we're all the same
Don't make fun, it's not a game.
It doesn't matter what you do
Making fun's not good for you.
Let's make this world a better place
For me and you, one human race.
Let's try to stop all of this
And live our lives in peaceful bliss.

Harley Beckett (11)
Winterhill School, Kimberworth

Bullying

B e nice to other people
U nderstand how they feel
L ike everyone no matter who they are
L ove them, care for them
Y ou should respect them
I should respect them
N ow everybody listen
G et along with everyone.

Jamie Lee Holmes (12)
Winterhill School, Kimberworth

You Big Bully!

I'm the one who is not cool
I'm the one who is a fool.
Everyone bullied me to look cool
But I think they are the fool.

For a while they went away
But it was only for a day.
When I went to school
They thought I wasn't cool.

You may be dim, you may be bright
Because it is alright.
This is the time to play
This is going to be a good day!

Aiman Chaudhary (12)
Winterhill School, Kimberworth

Bullying Is Bad

Bullying is bad
You're not a hard lad
If you get hit
Don't have a fit.

Bullying is bad
Go tell your dad
You can't cope
Don't just hope.

Bullying is bad
Be a good lad
You're not cool
Don't be a fool.

James Jessop (12)
Winterhill School, Kimberworth

Personalities

Whether you're black, white, pink or green
Big, small, mucky or clean
You're you, that's all you need to be,
Just use your personality.
If you are being bullied,
It is because the bullies are jealous of what you've got,
Don't worry, you're you, that's all you need to be,
Just use your personality.
Names are ways of getting to you,
Just ignore them, that's what I'd do,
Remember, you're you, that's all you need to be,
Use your personality.
Whether you've got no hair or lots and lots
Or if you have got some spots
You are you, that's all you need to be,
Use your personality.

Rosie Adams (12)
Winterhill School, Kimberworth

Bullying

All this violence,
Why should we be silenced?
We shouldn't stand for this.
Make the world a better place
Don't let them stand on your lace
Because bullying is bad,
You're not a bad lad
So let's put a stop to this
And start some hip hop.

Thomas Knowles (12)
Winterhill School, Kimberworth

We're Against It Together

Black and white, we're all the same,
All of us have different names.
All may come from different places
And we all have different faces,
Let's just get on with one another
And make them feel like your brother.
Let's make this world a better place
And live together as one race,
Let's try and stop all of this
And let's get on with Sir and Miss.
Don't turn yourself into a bully
As we'll all get along together fully.

Oliver Varnam (12)
Winterhill School, Kimberworth

Colour Poem

Green is the colour of the trees I live in.
Black is the colour of the trees after a fire
Blue is the colour of the sky.
White is the colour of my tail.
Red is the colour of anger.
Purple is the colour of when I am in a good mood.

Bethany Turton (13)
Winterhill School, Kimberworth

Bullying

Bullying is wrong
Bullying is bad
Go and tell your mum or dad
Altogether play games
Instead of calling names.

Charlie Goodwin (12)
Winterhill School, Kimberworth

Bullying

When I was at school
I never had friends
They started to bully me
And now it never ends.

Every break and dinner
I am always alone
I always thought, *why don't they just
Fall and break a bone.*

They always teased me
In their little gang
Then one day
I heard a *bang!*

In his hand he had a gun
A bullet in my head
Then before I knew it
I was there, dead!

Josh Chaim (12)
Winterhill School, Kimberworth

Torture From A Bully

Bullies are bad
Bullies are mean
I'd be full of pride
And bullies would kill it all.

Bullies are bad
Bullies are mean
I get so sad
A day in my life is worthless.

Bullies are bad
Bullies are mean
It gets too much
I die in my room.

Joe Blamire (11)
Winterhill School, Kimberworth

Endangered Animals

S ome species of
A nimals are becoming
V ery close to
E xtinction

T hey don't have help
H ow can they survive alone
E very day

A nimals that are
N ot able to cope
I n-between life and death
M aybe you could help these
A nimals that need your
L ove and
S upport.

Danny Birch (13)
Winterhill School, Kimberworth

Bullying Hurts!

Bullying is very hurtful to people
Bullying can be racist and everything else
Bullying can be loads of things.

Racism is very upsetting to people
Racism is not very polite
Racism can be loads of things.

Peer pressure makes people want to hurt themselves
Peer pressure makes people mad
Peer pressure gives you a bad life.

Josh Steer (12)
Winterhill School, Kimberworth

Stop Bullying Now

B ullying is not nice
U nkind
L ow life
L onely
Y oung
I f you don't ignore them they will carry on
N obody knows what could happen
G et help, get advice.

Sam Pepper (11)
Winterhill School, Kimberworth

Bullying Is Bad

Bullying is bad
It makes people sad
If you get hit
Don't have a fit

Bullying is bad
If you're not a hard lad
Bullying is bad
It makes people sad.

Liam Moore (12)
Winterhill School, Kimberworth

We Will Stand Strong Together

We are all equal
We shine like stars
Our lives are important
Don't be trapped behind the bars
As we all go out to play
Together we are like sunshine on a rainy day.

Rosanna Scarlett (12)
Winterhill School, Kimberworth

Before And After

I was being bullied
It made me feel sad
I did not know what to do
I told my dad

After that it all came to an end
I felt a lot happier
I made some friends

If you are being bullied
Ask for help, tell someone
You will stop being worried.

Amy Moody (12)
Winterhill School, Kimberworth

About Bullying

Bullying is bad
It makes other people sad.
Kicking, punching, calling names,
All together play lots of games.
Play together like best friends
Help each other make lots of dens.
Life is good to you
Make friends that are new.
Tell your teacher and dad or mum
There is a life ahead of you so have some fun!

Rebecca Lousie Dodds (12)
Winterhill School, Kimberworth

Bullying Is Over

We are all equal
We are all the same
Let's get on together
Or our lives will be in pain.

Mollie Quinn (12)
Winterhill School, Kimberworth

Endangered Earth

The Earth is dying
Save it quick
All the destruction
Makes me sick
Seals, tigers
And monkeys too,
To save the animals
All you have to do
Is stop the hunting
Stop it now
Save the Earth
Then take a bow
You just saved lives
You should be proud
You kept the tiger
Roaring out loud
Save the creatures
For the animal kingdom
Set them free
And give them freedom
Save the planet
It could be us next!

Chris Potts (12)
Winterhill School, Kimberworth

Let's Stop Bullying

Bullying is wrong
Hold your tongue
Don't answer back
You'll get a smack
Ignore what they do
I'm sure you'll get through.

Louis Booth (11)
Winterhill School, Kimberworth

Tigers And Lions

T igers strolling in the jungle
I n the blazing heat
G oing near to a village
E verybody's scared
R acing about the village then it goes back to its home

A nimals
N othing's stopping them becoming extinct
D ying in the heat

L ightning quick
I thought of his deeds
O h they're coming, his enemies
N othing can stop him
S ickeningly he strikes his enemies down.

Kieran Ruane (12)
Winterhill School, Kimberworth

Bullying Is Wrong

Bullying is wrong
Try to get along
Try to all be friends.

You should try
Don't sigh
It is much better.

Then no one is sad
Don't make each other mad
Be a good lad.

Natalie Jones (11)
Winterhill School, Kimberworth

Beat The Bullies

I'm the person you laughed at when I cried
That is when my social life died.
You laughed at me and called me lame
I pity you cos you're all the same.

People bully me just for fun
They're not clever, they're just dumb.
They look me up and down and have nothing to say
It's funny how the words come out when I walk away.

They bully me just to look cool
Why am I always the one who looks like a fool?
One day I stood up to him, he didn't now what was going on
He knew not to tease me anymore, now I'm not the one!

Jessica Hoden (12)
Winterhill School, Kimberworth

Stamp Out Bullying

I'm the person you joked about all the time
You're the people who made me put my life on the line.
You're in your gang acting all cool
When even though you're the one who really is the fool!
I wish I could find the key
Because I never hear a joke unless the joke's about me!
They hit me, my skin turned black
I didn't know what to do; I wanted to hit them back.
Come on people, we are all the same
We need to stand up to them cos they're putting us in pain.

Kallum Stanley (11)
Winterhill School, Kimberworth

Don't Bully

Do not bully, it is not right,
It could get you into a fight.
Black or white, we're all the same,
Don't say anything or you'll get the blame.
Pretty, ugly, fat or thin,
Just be nice or you're in the bin.
Don't call people names
Just play gentle games.
Friendship is the best thing ever
So let's all be nice together.

Katherine Dawn Holley (12)
Winterhill School, Kimberworth

Young Writers Information

We hope you have enjoyed reading this book - and that you will continue to enjoy it in the coming years.

If you like reading and writing poetry drop us a line, or give us a call, and we'll send you a free information pack.

Alternatively if you would like to order further copies of this book or any of our other titles, then please give us a call or log onto our website at www.youngwriters.co.uk

**Young Writers Information
Remus House
Coltsfoot Drive
Peterborough
PE2 9JX**

(01733) 890066